# The Book
## of
# GREAT
# INVENTIONS

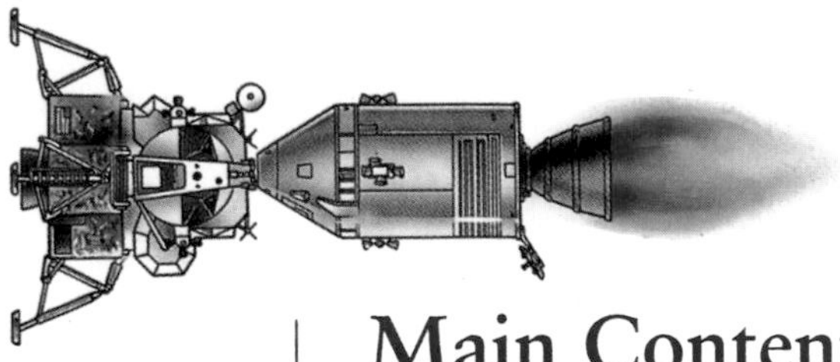

This edition produced
in 1995 for
**Shooting Star Press Inc**
230 Fifth Avenue
Suite 1212
New York, NY 10001

© Aladdin Books Ltd 1995

Designed and produced by
Aladdin Books Ltd
28 Percy Street
London W1P 0LD

Printed in Italy

ISBN 1-57335-147-4

*Some of the material in
this book was previously
published in the
Inventions in Science series.*

# Main Contents

# The Book of GREAT INVENTIONS

WRITTEN BY

CHRIS OXLADE, STEVE PARKER, NIGEL HAWKES

ILLUSTRATED BY

DAVID RUSSELL, IAN THOMPSON

SHOOTING STAR PRESS

# INTRODUCTION

What would life be like today without cars, planes or boats? This book looks at the origins and development of the inventions that have transformed the modern world. Each chapter examines the science and technology behind the invention, and explores its impact on everyday life.

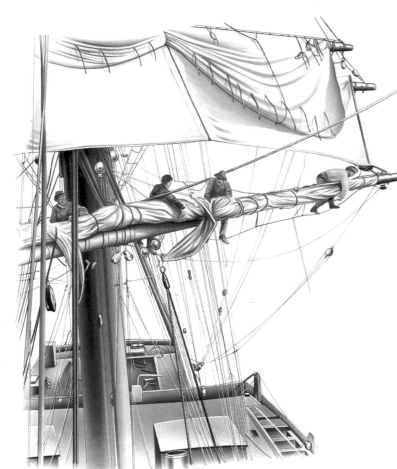

## Ships and Boats

Humans have used ships and boats as a form of transport for thousands of years. Starting as simple floating logs, shipping technology has grown and expanded beyond recognition, creating a dazzling array of ships, each with a specific task. These range from simple pleasure craft, to massive super-tankers, and the ultra-modern warships that guard our coasts.

## Flying Machines

The mystery of flight has amazed humanity for centuries, and yet it has only been achieved in the last one hundred years. This chapter examines the early attempts at flight, the first successes, the development of the jet engine, and the never-ending quest for speed that has taken planes to the speed of sound, and beyond.

# The Car

The arrival of the internal combustion engine, and with it the car, has totally changed the way we live, and the world we live in. Since the early days of motor transport, the car has taken over. Vehicles are available for all, cutting journey times. However, massive roads now cut swathes across the countryside, and the vehicles themselves produce millions of tons of chemicals that poison our atmosphere.

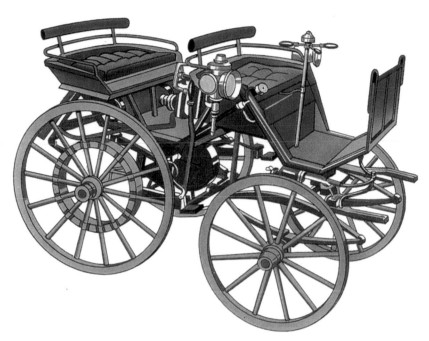

# Into Space

On October 4, 1957, the launch of a small metal sphere, called Sputnik 1 into orbit, started the Space Age. In the forty years since then, humans have set foot on another planet, have sent probes around the solar system and beyond. The future will see the construction of a space station, and a possible mission to Mars.

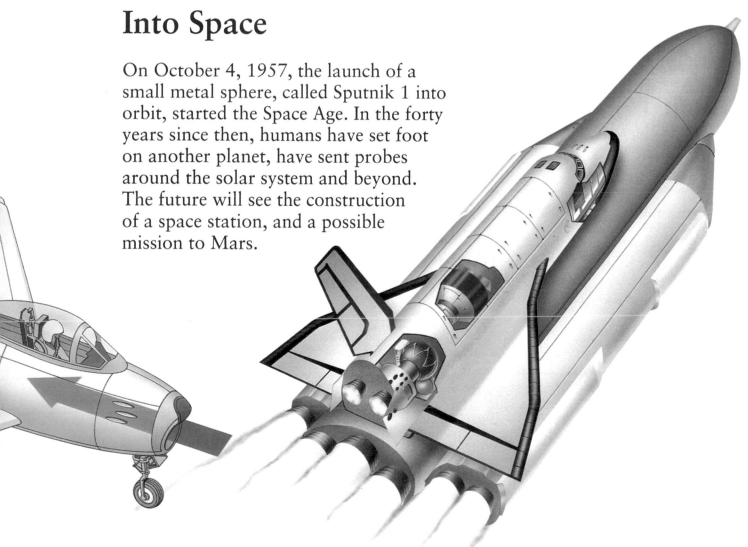

# The Book of GREAT INVENTIONS

# SHIPS
## AND BOATS

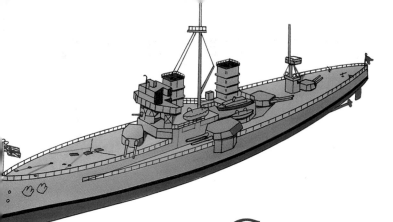

# CONTENTS

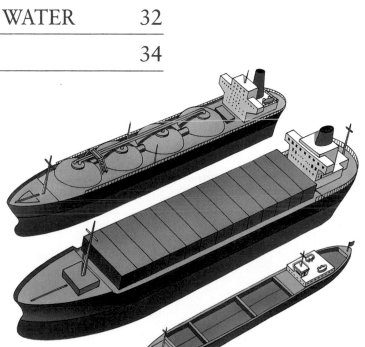

# SHIPS TODAY

Ships and boats are the oldest forms of transport. They were invented many thousands of years ago, and have developed slowly since then. Today, ships and boats play an important part in our lives, for travel, leisure, defense, fishing, and most important of all, international trade. Over 75 per cent of international cargo is carried from country to country across oceans and seas, and along inland waterways. This is the story of the invention of the boat, of the many technological improvements that have taken place, and of the impact that these advances have had on our own lives.

A modern hydrofoil on its skis.

**Oil tankers**
Oil tankers are the giants of the shipping world. They have their own special terminals for loading and unloading.

**Containers**
Specially built container ships load and unload directly onto lorries.

**Ferries**
Many ferries carry people and vehicles, as well as freight, across water.

**Fishing boats**
Many of today's modern ports started as fishing harbors. Today, they often maintain a fleet of fishing boats.

**Lifeboats**
Self-righting, offshore lifeboats are a vital part of coastal rescue.

**Warships**
Naval warships are used to protect a country's territorial waters and to look after its sea-trade routes.

**Hovercraft**
A hovercraft glides along a cushion of air and can operate along shallow waters as well as in open seas.

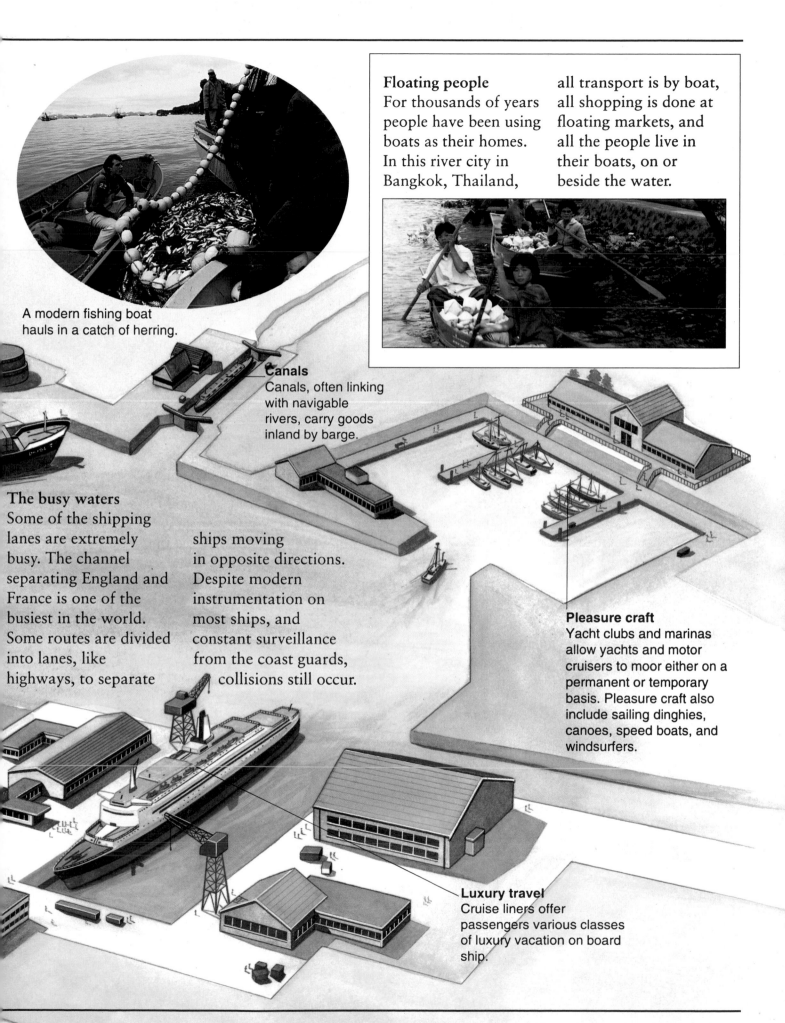

A modern fishing boat hauls in a catch of herring.

### Floating people

For thousands of years people have been using boats as their homes. In this river city in Bangkok, Thailand, all transport is by boat, all shopping is done at floating markets, and all the people live in their boats, on or beside the water.

### Canals

Canals, often linking with navigable rivers, carry goods inland by barge.

### The busy waters

Some of the shipping lanes are extremely busy. The channel separating England and France is one of the busiest in the world. Some routes are divided into lanes, like highways, to separate ships moving in opposite directions. Despite modern instrumentation on most ships, and constant surveillance from the coast guards, collisions still occur.

### Pleasure craft

Yacht clubs and marinas allow yachts and motor cruisers to moor either on a permanent or temporary basis. Pleasure craft also include sailing dinghies, canoes, speed boats, and windsurfers.

### Luxury travel

Cruise liners offer passengers various classes of luxury vacation on board ship.

# THE FIRST CRAFT

The first craft were probably logs, bundles of reeds, or inflated animal skins, bound together to form a raft. Archaeological evidence suggests that the ancestors of the Aborigines first landed in Australia using sea-going rafts, many thousands of years before "real" boats were built. The first true boat (a watertight structure in which a person can sit) was probably a hollowed-out log. The discovery that such objects could float in water was made in many parts of the world. This led to a variety of boats from dugouts and bark canoes to plank boats. Many of these are still used around the world today.

*Ra II*

**Egyptian rafts**

Egyptian drawings on clay tablets show rafts constructed from bundles of papyrus tied together. They were used on the Nile River from about 7,000 B.C. and were important in the development of Ancient Egypt.

*Ra II*

In 1970, Thor Heyerdahl, the Norwegian anthropologist, sailed his *Ra II*, made of papyrus reeds, from Africa to the West Indies. He did this to show that it would have been possible for the early seafarers to undertake great journeys across the Atlantic as long ago as three or four thousand years.

**Coracles**

The coracle (left) is still used for fishing on certain rivers in Wales today. Originally, a thin frame was covered by animal skins, but this has been replaced by tar-covered canvas today. The quffa basket boats are used on the rivers Tigris and Euphrates in Iraq. Unlike the tiny coracle they can hold as many as twenty people.

North American Indian canoe

### Dugouts

Dugout canoes were one of the earliest forms of simple boat. Hollowed out from a tree trunk, they were shaped and streamlined to give increased speed. The outrigger canoes of the Pacific islands are still based on the dugout principle.

A plank boat under construction in Oman.

### Early sailing ships

Ships with square sails were being used in 3,000 B.C. by the Egyptians for long sea voyages. The triangular or lateen sail was first invented by the Arabs during the Middle Ages. In China, junks (below) featured multiple masts and a rudder, several centuries before European ships.

### Bark canoes

Bark canoes are faster and lighter than dugouts. The bark is stripped from a large tree in one piece and stretched over a wooden framework. Bark canoes were made extensively by the North American Indians and this method is still practiced by the Aborigines of Australia.

### Plank boats

By joining timbers together, a boat can be made bigger and stronger. Most plank boats are built with timbers attached to a central frame. The timbers either overlay each other or are fastened edge to edge. The Viking longboat was an early example of a plank boat. It was built with overlapping planks attached to a very strong keel. They were amazingly strong, making it possible for the Vikings to make long voyages across the Atlantic, and even as far as Newfoundland.

Viking Longboat

### The past today

Many of the boats discussed here (the coracle, quffa, bark canoe) are still used today. Boats such as modern windsurfers and kayaks are made of modern materials such as fiberglass or plastic, but the original shape and design still remain the same today.

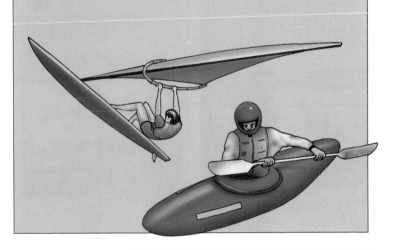

# THE AGE OF SAILING

During the Middle Ages, the Arabs were the outstanding seafarers. With two-masted dhows and lateen-rigged sails (triangular sails that made better use of different winds), they ventured as far as Africa and China. In the 1450s, the Northern Europeans developed their own two- and three-masted ships. Their wooden, rounded hulls were built around strong keels and they were able to cross the oceans. New continents were discovered, leading to a surge of trade in exotic new products like spices and tobacco.

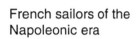

French sailors of the Napoleonic era

## Life on board

The ships were small, the work was hard, and the conditions harsh. Crews had to survive for months on a diet of salted beef and biscuits without fresh food, resulting in many deaths from the disease scurvy.

## Great ships

The first "great" warships were built on the orders of Henry VIII of England (1509-1547). Although the *Mary Rose* sank because her guns made her top heavy, this style of warship was to last for nearly 300 years.

## The galleon

Until 1588, most warships were propelled by a combination of sails and oars. During the Armada of 1588, Sir Walter Raleigh and his English fleet of three-masted sailing galleons repulsed the Spanish invasion fleet, using sails only.

## Ship-of-the-line

From 1650 to 1850 the ship-of-the-line reigned supreme. These sailing battleships could deliver the maximum firing power against the enemy. They were rated by the number of guns they carried. The first-rate *Victory* (right) had 104 guns on three main gun decks.

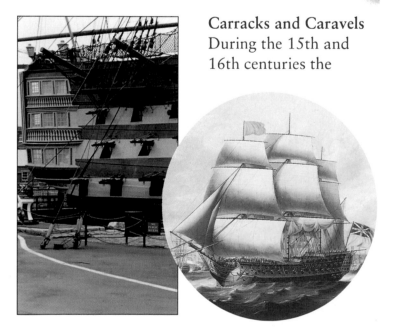

## Carracks and Caravels

During the 15th and 16th centuries the Spanish and Portuguese carrack became the standard large European ship. With up to 4 masts, the carrack was a tough ocean-going merchantman. Smaller than a carrack, the caravel could either be sailed across seas or rowed by oarsmen in shallow waters.

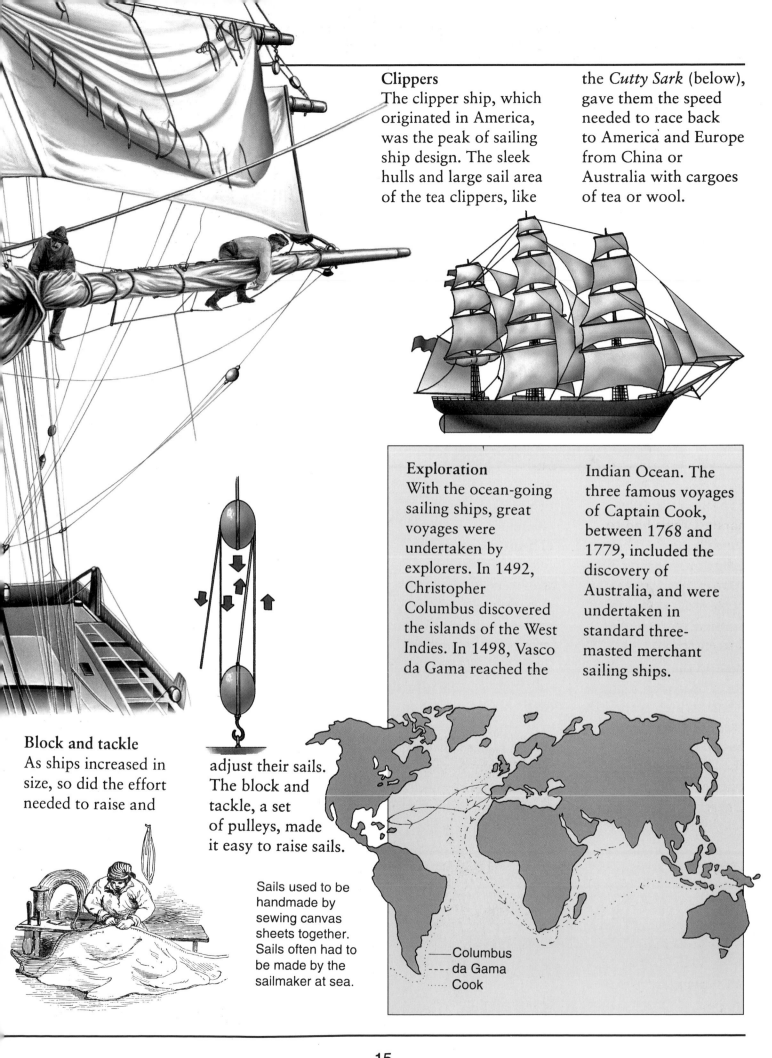

## Clippers

The clipper ship, which originated in America, was the peak of sailing ship design. The sleek hulls and large sail area of the tea clippers, like the *Cutty Sark* (below), gave them the speed needed to race back to America and Europe from China or Australia with cargoes of tea or wool.

## Exploration

With the ocean-going sailing ships, great voyages were undertaken by explorers. In 1492, Christopher Columbus discovered the islands of the West Indies. In 1498, Vasco da Gama reached the Indian Ocean. The three famous voyages of Captain Cook, between 1768 and 1779, included the discovery of Australia, and were undertaken in standard three-masted merchant sailing ships.

—— Columbus
- - - da Gama
······· Cook

## Block and tackle

As ships increased in size, so did the effort needed to raise and adjust their sails. The block and tackle, a set of pulleys, made it easy to raise sails.

Sails used to be handmade by sewing canvas sheets together. Sails often had to be made by the sailmaker at sea.

# THE STEAM LINER

The invention of the steam engine triggered the Industrial Revolution. Not only were ships no longer dependent on the wind, but the new processes for making iron meant that larger and larger hulls could be constructed with greater strength. Steam engines improved, coal became available around the world, and propellers were invented. The S.S. *Great Britain*, designed and built by Isambard Brunel, was the first iron-hulled and propeller-driven ship to cross the Atlantic. The *Great Eastern*, also designed by Brunel, at 30,690 tons was by far the largest ship built at the time. Launched in 1858, it was a commercial failure.

**The steam engine**
James Watt (above) developed the first efficient steam engine. Water, heated by coal, generated steam which expanded and caused the piston to move. The piston then moved the beam through a crank-shaft, which turned the paddle wheel or pulley to drive the screw.

**The first steamers**
The first steamships were small paddle-steamers, such as the *Charlotte Dundas*, the first commercially successful steamer launched in 1802. As the huge wheels turned, their blades dipped in the water, pushing the vessel along. They were most useful for shallow waters, and the largest river boat (which is still going strong) is the *Mississippi Queen*.

**Emigration**
The first real emigrants, the Pilgrim Fathers, reached America in 1620 on sailing ships like the *Mayflower*. Between 1820 and 1920, an estimated 35 million people crossed the Atlantic to America. The great steam liners offered them cheap, if sometimes uncomfortable, passage.

## Paddle vs screw

The first steamships all used paddles for propulsion. The screw propeller was invented in 1836, but it took some time to replace the paddle wheel. In 1845, the British Admiralty staged a contest between H.M.S. *Rattler* (propellers) and H.M.S. *Alecto* (paddle wheels). H.M.S. *Rattler* won easily, pulling the paddle steamer backwards through the water.

The *QE2* is one of the few remaining luxury liners, seen here leaving Albert Dock in Liverpool, England.

SS *Great Britain* 3,288 tons. Designed by Brunel, it was the first ocean-going liner to be made of iron and driven by a propeller. Maiden voyage, 1845.

## The first liners

At first, the range of steam-powered ships was limited. The English engineer, Brunel, built the *Great Western*. A paddle steamer weighing 1,477 tons, it was big enough to hold enough fuel and fresh water needed for long trips. Although it was not the first ship to cross the Atlantic under steam power alone, it was the first real transatlantic liner.

## The golden age of liners

By 1914, luxury liners of 45,000 tons or more were crossing the Atlantic in just five days. The invention of the steam turbine in 1894 by Charles Parsons, had led to the increase in power required for such liners. In the 1930s, the grandest way to cross the Atlantic was by luxury liner. By the 1950's, however, these great ships, despite their luxury, could no longer compete with the new era of jetliners.

## The Blue Riband

Shipping lines for transatlantic passengers competed for this trophy to be the fastest across the Atlantic. The Blue Riband was awarded to many great liners, including the *Mauretania*, which held the record for 22 years.

## The *Titanic*

The *Titanic* was claimed to be the "unsinkable" liner of the White Star Line. On her maiden (first) voyage in 1912 she was crossing the Atlantic on a more northerly route than was normal when she hit an iceberg. More than 1,500 of the 2,200 people on board were lost, many because there were not enough lifeboats.

# THE POWER

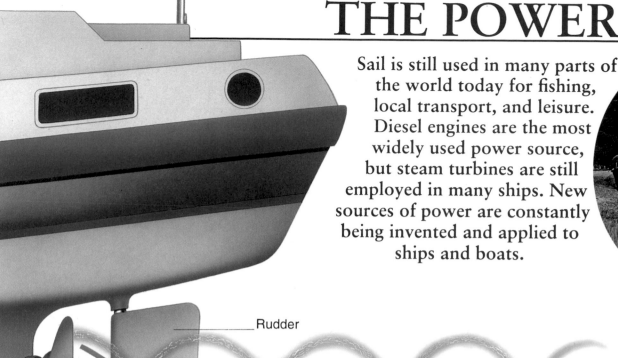

Sail is still used in many parts of the world today for fishing, local transport, and leisure. Diesel engines are the most widely used power source, but steam turbines are still employed in many ships. New sources of power are constantly being invented and applied to ships and boats.

Rudder

Propeller

## The propeller

The propeller or screw is designed to convert engine power into forward or backward motion. Angled blades of the propeller rotate, pushing against the water and moving the boat along. The angle of the screw is called the pitch.

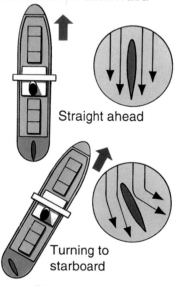

Straight ahead

Turning to starboard

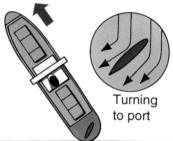

Turning to port

## Steering

Until the 15th century, most steering was done with an oar tied to the back of the ship. The turning of the rudder alters the flow of water pushing the stern of the ship sideways and causes the boat to turn to port or starboard. Bow thrusters worked by water jets or propellers can assist large ships to maneuver, particularly when in port.

## Stabilizers

Stabilizers reduce rolling in rough seas. They are used to make passenger ships more comfortable, to prevent cargo moving, and to create a level missile platform or landing area on naval ships. Altering the angle of the stabilizer (or aerofoil) will either lower or raise that side of the ship.

Stabilizer

Hull

Direction of roll

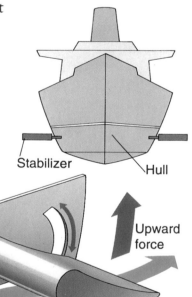

Upward force

## Water jets

Water is drawn in at the front and pumped out at high pressure through jets causing forward propulsion of the boat. They may be used for the silent propulsion of submarines or to power hydrofoils like the one shown below.

## The diesel engine

Invented by the German, Rudolf Diesel, the diesel engine is widely used in ships and boats of all sizes, like the giant P&O container ship (top right). Continuous low speed running and fuel economy are the hallmarks of the diesel engine. A diesel engine is used by the Finnish ice-breaker (bottom right) because of its great power.

Hydrofoil

## Turbines

In many ships, fuel oil is burned to make steam for turbine propulsion. In a gas turbine, fuel and air are burned under great pressure to turn a series of turbine vanes. These are geared to rotate the propeller shaft. Gas turbines are suitable for ships that require higher speeds than normal, for example, frigates and torpedo boats.

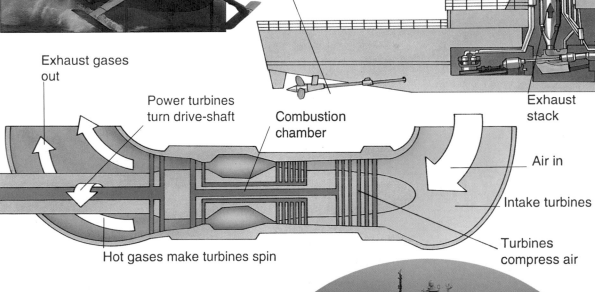

Propeller shaft

Exhaust gases out

Power turbines turn drive-shaft

Combustion chamber

Exhaust stack

Air in

Intake turbines

Turbines compress air

Hot gases make turbines spin

## Nuclear power

The first nuclear-powered ship, *Savannah*, was launched in 1959. At the time it was thought that this was the power source of the future - *Savannah* needed refueling only every two years. However, the huge development costs, and later the awareness of the hazards of nuclear power, mean that it has never been widely used for merchant ships. Today, nuclear power is limited mainly to aircraft carriers and large submarines.

Finnish ice-breaker

# CARGO

The transportation of cargo has always been one of the main driving forces behind boat and ship development. The Roman Empire relied on a network of shipping routes around the Mediterranean, and the development of ocean-going craft saw the spectacular expansion of trading routes. Today, it is the most cost effective way of transporting cargo over long distances. Until recently, cargo ships tended to be "general purpose," carrying a wide range of goods. Today, although coastal freight still carries local cargo, ships have become much more specialized.

A barge in Thailand being towed slowly along the river. Whole families use the barge as a home.

### The East India Company

The East India Company was one of the most successful trading companies of the seventeenth century. Trade with countries in the Far East gave rise to a new kind of ship – the East Indiaman – a fast, heavily armored cargo ship.

### Trade expansion

Trade increased rapidly during the Industrial Revolution. Ships could be constructed from iron, they became bigger, and steam made them, faster. Some clipper ships still operated into the 1930s. The first oil tanker was launched in 1885.

Double hull

Stabilizer

### Pollution

In March 1989, the *Exxon Valdez* ran aground in Prince William Sound, Alaska. It spilled millions of gallons of crude oil into the sea, polluting over 250 miles of Alaskan coastline and killing millions of fish and seabirds. In 1993, the *Braer* (below) ran aground in the Shetlands, Scotland, spilling its cargo of oil. This time, damage to wildlife appears to have been limited.

### Giants of the sea

Oil tankers are by far the largest ships afloat. Despite their huge size, oil tankers are of a relatively simple construction. They often require a flotilla of tugs to maneuver them at their special terminals. The recent spate of tanker accidents resulted in demands for greater safety standards, including the fitting of a double-skinned hull to future tankers.

The containerization of freight into standard size units has revolutionized cargo-carrying vessels. Huge container vessels load and unload at terminals with special handling equipment. These giant ships now gross more than 50,000 tons and can travel at an amazing 24 knots (27 mph). They may carry up to four thousand containers.

Satellite equipment helps rescue services to locate the tanker.

## Load lines

Load lines, or Plimsoll lines, are marks on the side of the ship to show how a vessel is floating in the water. They indicate how much can be loaded onto a ship in different sea conditions. This safety standard has been compulsory on merchant ships for over a hundred years.

Tankers like the one below gross over 400,000 tons and are over 1,150ft long.

Tankers like this are called ULCC - Ultra Large Crude Carrier.

RoRo

Bulk carrier

Gas carrier

Bulk carrier

Barge

## Different types

Roll-on-Roll-off (RoRo) ferries are designed with large fitting doors at both ends to allow the vehicles to drive on and off. Bulk carriers, suitable for coal and grain, have a number of large cargo holds. Gas carriers transport liquid gas in pressurized or refrigerated tanks. Barges, both sea-going and inland, are used extensively to take cargo from the main freight terminals to their final destinations inland.

# PORTS AND HARBORS

Ports were originally sheltered places where boats could land safely away from the stormy seas. Often, natural harbors occur in rivers, bays, and estuaries, and are home to fleets of fishing boats. As trade by sea expanded, the population of the small ports grew, as did facilities such as wharves, wharehouses, tugs, cranes, and railway and truck transportation. Many of the world's largest cities have grown up around their ports. Some, like New York, have retained their importance, but others, like London, England, have seen a decline in shipping activities.

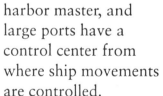

### Natural harbors
Tenby, Wales (above) is a typical small sheltered harbor with its flotilla of small fishing boats, sailing dingies, and motorboats.
Natural harbors are found in deep water inlets protected from waves and wind.

### Sailing cities
Founded in 1924 by Dutch traders, New York has always been the United States' busiest port. It is shown here in the heyday of transatlantic liners. Today, New York is still one of the busiest seaports in the world.

### The harbor master
As ships arrive at port, they need to be berthed before loading or unloading as quickly as possible. The efficient running of a port is the responsibility of the harbor master, and large ports have a control center from where ship movements are controlled.

Coal being unloaded at the port of Antwerp, Belgium.

Special container terminal   Crane

Containers

**Container ports**
Special terminals handle only containers. They are loaded on and off ships, often onto waiting lorries and trains.

**The final destination**
These barges on the Rhine in Germany (above) collected cargo from the major port of Rotterdam and are on their way to their final destination. Trucks also collect containers from the port, and transport the goods to the next destination.

**The modern port**
Antwerp, shown below, is typical of a modern port. Ships of every size and description are loaded and unloaded with sophisticated cranes and elevators. Antwerp is unusual in that it is the largest inland port in the world, being some 55 miles from the nearest coastline.

Rail link

**Tugs and pilot boats**
Every large harbor has a pilot service. Pilots have detailed knowledge of the port approaches and harbor layout, and take the "helm" on ships as they arrive and depart. Tugs (right) assist vessels to maneuver at low speeds.

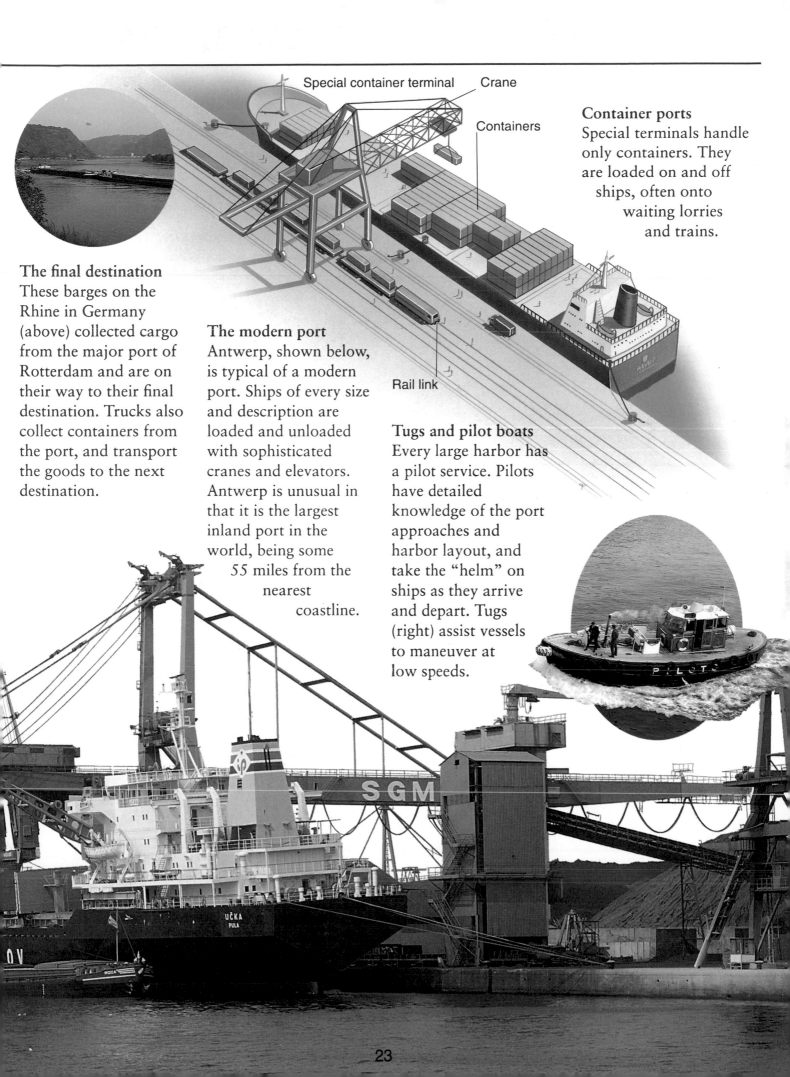

# SHIPBUILDING

Shipyards changed as ships got bigger and iron and steel replaced wood. After mammoth shipbuilding programs in the early 1900s, there was a further expansion after World War II as a new generation of aircraft carriers, submarines, container boats, and tankers were developed. Today, the airplane takes most of the passengers who once used the Atlantic liners. There are too many ships floating with no cargoes, world trade is stagnant, and there is little enthusiasm for building yet more warships.

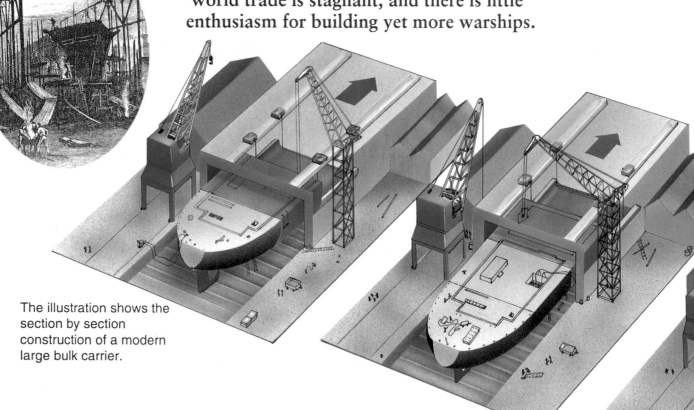

The illustration shows the section by section construction of a modern large bulk carrier.

## The old way

The illustration at the top of the page shows a boat being constructed on the Tyne River, England in about 1880. The plate shell is being riveted onto the structure in the same way as the planks of a wooden boat are attached. Today, shipbuilding relies on a large workforce, specialized in riveting, boiler-making and welding. When the hull is launched, the ship will have most of the main parts built. Once afloat, the ship is pulled into an outfitting dock where it will be fitted out to the customer's requirements. This involves adding the electrical systems, navigational aids, safety items, works, and furnishings. The ship will then undergo extensive sea trials and be brought into service.

The traditional method of building boats around a "chassis" is still used in this Arab shipyard (below) where models are being built.

## Shipbuilding today

Until 1945, most iron ships had metal plates around a structure that had already been built. Modern ships of size are made of box-like structures, with metal plates and girders welded together. Bulkheads running across, and up and down the ship strengthen the construction, and divide the ship up into separate watertight compartments. This helps to prevent the entire flooding of the ship if one compartment is holed. The illustration (below) shows the stages of construction of a typical large bulk carrier. Large prefabricated sections are lifted and secured into place one section at a time. As one section is completed, the overhead cranes move to the next section, allowing other workers to add engines and deck fittings to the previous section. Once complete, the hull is launched down the shipway.

## Tank tests

Tank tests are used to check the designer's predictions about the ship's behavior. Wave machines in the tank can simulate any sea conditions, and the model can be moved through the water at different speeds and with different cargo loadings. The tank tests in the illustration are being carried out in Grenoble, France.

## Shipyard closures

Shipyards are often the major employer in port cities. Too many ships and the emergence of Japan and Korea as the leading shipbuilders has lead to the closure of many American and European shipyards.

## Computer design

Today, marine architects use computerized design. Drawings of the new ship are penciled in. The computer can calculate details of the new ship, and actually design the specification for the shipbuilder.

# NAVIGATION AND SAFETY

As sea lanes have become busier, ships have become bigger and faster, and their cargoes, in some cases, more hazardous. Never has the need for increased safety standards and better navigation been more important. Navigation aids consist of those on board ships such as radar, radio, and charts, assisted by satellites, and those which mark safe channels and warn of dangers, such as lighthouses and buoyage systems. Safety concerns not only the sea-worthiness of the vessel, but the standards of safety the crew are trained to operate. Although there are international safety agreements, some shipowners and masters manage to bypass them.

Ships carry a red light on the port side and a green light on starboard.

## Early navigation

Early ocean explorers used the sun and stars to judge which way they were going. The first navigational aid was the compass, used in Europe from about 1200 A.D. It consisted of a magnified needle mounted on a floating cork to show the ship's heading. The astrolabe, later replaced by the sextant (above), indicates a ship's north/south position.

## Busy waterways

The Strait of Singapore, on the main route for oil tankers from the Far East to Japan, is just 2 nautical miles (2.5 miles) wide. On average, 150 ships pass through every day. As straits like this become more and more congested, ships rely on navigational aids to avoid accidents and collisions.

Sonic depth finder measures depth of water.

## Buoyage systems

Buoyage systems are used to mark safe channels and hazards. Buoys were first used in the sixteenth century. Red and green buoys mark either side of a channel, using flashing lights in the dark.

Buoy with radar deflector

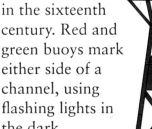

## Navigation today

Navigation has been made very simple by the invention of electronic aids. Radar and sonar locate other ships and underwater hazards. A ship's position is calculated automatically by radio or satellite navigation systems.

The Loran and Decca systems work by detecting the time difference between radio signals from shore-based radio stations. The NAVSTAR navigation system is a global positioning system (GPS). A receiver picks up signals from a network of satellites, and can calculate the ship's position to within 300 feet.

Satellites beam radio signals to Earth.

Lighthouse

Radar

## Lighthouses

The earliest known lighthouse was built in about 285 B.C. Electric poweer replaced naked flames in 1862. Tofay, many are completely automatic.

## Disaster

Going to sea always involves some risk. Bad weather will always claim ships and lives, but human error is responsible for many losses. The *Herald of Free Enterprise* capsized in the North Sea in 1987, killing over 200 people. When the ship left the port of Zeebrugge, the loading doors were left open. Water poured into the hold, unbalancing the ship.

## Lifeboats

Offshore lifeboats are designed with a watertight cabin and the engine low in the hull. This makes them very stable in rough seas. If they do capsize, trapped air in the cabin makes them bob back upright.

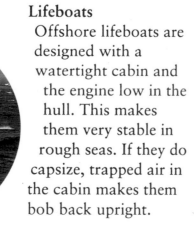

# FIGHTING SHIPS

Fighting ships were conceived as fighting platforms for troops to board and capture the enemy vessels. The early Egyptian galleys were probably the first real fighting ships, and although sails were added through the ages, galleys with banks of oarsmen were still in service until the 17th century. The great ships or galleons like the *Mary Rose* (which sank because she was made top heavy) were followed by the ships-of-the-line, like *Victory*. They used their broad sides of cannon fire to cripple opposing ships before boarding and capturing the enemy. The French *Gloire* (1859) was the first warship to carry iron armor plates, followed in 1860 by the English all-iron, screw-driven *Warrior*.

## Battleships

In *Warrior* (below), iron replaced wood, steam replaced sail, and guns replaced cannon. *Dreadnought* was one of the first new class of

battleships. It was launched in 1906, had ten 12-inch guns and a crew of 800 men. It was the first steam turbine-powered battleship.

HMS *Dreadnought*

## Triremes

The trireme (above) appeared in the Mediterranean around 500 B.C. A typical Greek trireme was about 130 ft long and 20 ft wide. It had three banks of oars operated by 170 oarsmen, and also carried warriors for combat. It attacked and sank other ships by ramming.

Fire control radar

Bridge

SAM launcher

Automatic gun

## Aircraft carriers

The first aircraft carriers were introduced between the two World Wars and during World War II they were the most important ship type.

Modern navies are based around aircraft carriers. The biggest carriers in the world are the *Nimitz* (below) class of the U.S. Navy. Their flight decks are 1,080 feet long and they carry about 90 aircraft and helicopters.

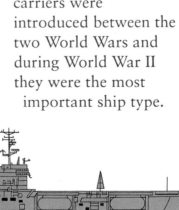

## New developments

High-tech developments are likely in naval craft. The U.S. Navy's *Sea Shadow*, shown left, can avoid detection by radar.

## Gunboat diplomacy

One of the main jobs of today's fighting ships is to wait near political trouble spots. This military "show of strength" known as "gunboat diplomacy" can be used to support or threaten. U.S.S. *Nimitz* is seen here displaying its airpower.

Long range search radar

Navigation radar

Target information radar

Fire control radar

Helicopter pad

H.M.S. Glasgow, a Sheffield (type 42) class destroyer.

Battleships in the Gulf conflict used their huge guns and launched cruise missiles.

## The modern ship

The use of iron and explosive shells revolutionized battleships. Modern fighting ships, such as the destroyer above, are fast, light, and crammed full of electronics. The gas turbine engines give it a top speed of 29 knots. Armament includes light guns, torpedoes, and surface-to-air (SAM) missiles for attacking aircraft. These are controlled by the computerized fire-control system. A helicopter is carried for antisubmarine operations. In a conflict, the ship's main role is to defend the fleet's aircraft carriers.

## High-speed boats

Some countries operate high-speed patrol boats around their coasts. They often include hydrofoils and hovercraft as well as gas turbine boats. Iranian gunboats sank several oil tankers in the Gulf with torpedoes, during the Iran/Iraq war of 1984/85.

# SUBMARINES

The submarine was invented as early as the 17th century, but it was not until the 1890s that American, John Holland, developed an effective power system using the internal combustion engine for surface propulsion and electricity when submerged. By 1914, greatly improved diesel engines and the introduction of torpedoes made the submarine a devastating weapon. The U-boat (Unterseeboot) wreaked havoc with Allied shipping during both World Wars, as did the American submarines against the Japanese. The ability of nuclear-powered submarines to stay underwater almost undetected, has made them the most deadly ships of all time.

The Turtle

Emergency breathing gear

## Early submarines

In 1620, Dutchman Cornelius von Drebbel built a wooden submarine. It was propelled by oars. The *Turtle*, built in 1775 by American, David Bushnell, was used during the American Revolution to try to sink a British frigate.

## How it works

Submarines dive and surface by filling and emptying their ballast tanks. Valves are opened to flood the tanks for diving, and compressed air is blown in to empty them for surfacing. The ship is "steered" with rudder-like hydroplanes.

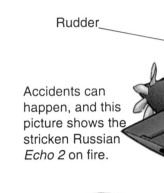

Rudder

Outer hull

Inner hull

Accidents can happen, and this picture shows the stricken Russian *Echo 2* on fire.

## Nuclear submarines

The first nuclear submarine, *Nautilus*, was launched by the U.S. Navy in 1955. The nuclear reactor's heat drives a steam turbine. No air is needed and the reactor can run for years without refueling. The submarine can stay submerged for many months at a time. This ability is essential for the ballistic missile submarines which carry nuclear deterrents, and the hunter-killers that are shadowing them.

## Escape to safety

In case of damage serious enough to prevent the submarine resurfacing, a submarine's crew put on emergency breathing equipment and leave via escape chambers. These are vertical tubes with watertight doors and an opening in the deck.

**Surfaced**

Air

Compressed air

**Surfacing**

Air in

Seawater

Valves open

Seawater out

**Diving**

Air out

**Submerged**

Valves closed

Seawater in

## Sonar

Sonar (or echo sounding) is a way of locating underwater objects. A speaker sends out a series of beeps into the water and a hydrophone (underwater microphone) detects echoes from objects. Sonar systems can also work in "passive" mode, locating surface ships by listening for their engine noises. Many submarines now have propulsion that runs "silently."

## The deepest dive

The deepest dive was made by the U.S. Navy's deep submergence vessel, *Sea Cliff* (shown above) in 1985. It reached a depth of 20,000 feet.

## Nuclear deterrent

Every day huge military submarines cruise silently and unseen in the world's oceans. These nuclear-powered ballistic missile submarines (SSBNs) carry their country's nuclear deterrent. Their presence is to prevent aggression from others.

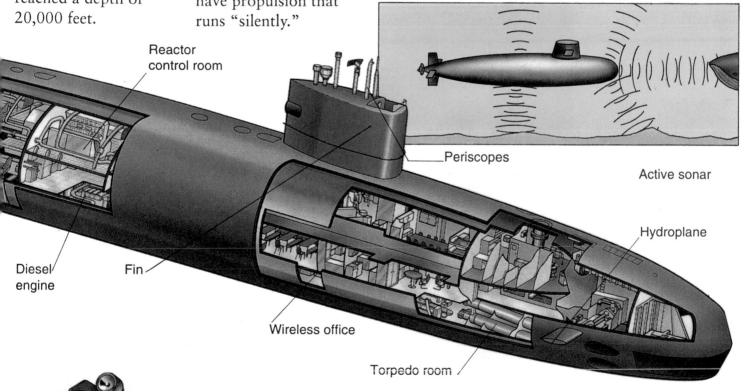

Reactor control room

Periscopes

Active sonar

Hydroplane

Diesel engine

Fin

Wireless office

Torpedo room

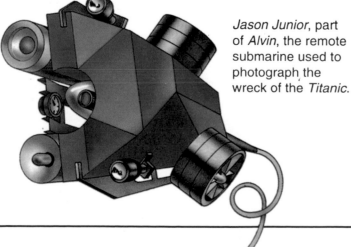

*Jason Junior*, part of *Alvin*, the remote submarine used to photograph the wreck of the *Titanic*.

## Robot submarines

Robot submarines are often used for simple underwater tasks, such as photographing a wreck. On board are TV cameras which relay pictures back to a control room on the surface vessel. The submarine is steered remotely from the surface with a joystick. The advantage of using a robot is that no crew is needed. This is not only safer, but means that the submarine can be much smaller and is much easier to build.

# LEISURE ON THE WATER

Boats have long been used for pleasure, relaxation, and sport. As the amount of leisure time available to people has increased, boating has become a popular sport and pastime. There are options for all tastes and budgets, from hiring a rowing boat in the local park, through racing a sailing yacht on the sea, to vacationing on a luxury motor cruiser.

A modern yacht

**Come in number 1**
Rowing a boat in the local park or on the river is an enjoyable pastime. Sailboarding or windsurfing (above) is a sport enjoyed by many people, on lakes, reservoirs, and at sea.

**Dinghy sailing**
Dinghy sailing is the way most people are introduced to sailing. Small dinghies are cheap to buy and easy to handle. Windsurfing is really a cross between dinghy sailing and surfing, and has become popular since it was invented about 20 years ago.

**Yachting and canoeing**
For many people, yachting is their way of experiencing the adventure of going to sea. In its simplest form, it is spending a day cruising in local waters. At the other end of the spectrum, it is taking part in the America's Cup or sailing single-handed around the world. Canoeing is also a popular sport. Canoes are easy to operate, maintain, store, and transport, and can be used on rivers, lakes, and the sea.

## Inland waterways

In some countries, cruising slowly along inland waterways and canals has become a popular vacation activity. A barge is a sturdy flat-bottomed boat which once carried bulk cargoes such as cement, coal, logs, and oil. Early barges were once pulled by horses, now they are powered by their own engines. Narrow canals which no longer carry commercial traffic are ideal – vacationers live on the boats and operate the canal locks for themselves.

Barge moored on a canal in Gloucestershire, England.

1. Lock is filled to level of top port.

2. Boat enters lock and water is let into bottom canal.

3. When water is level the boat can move out.

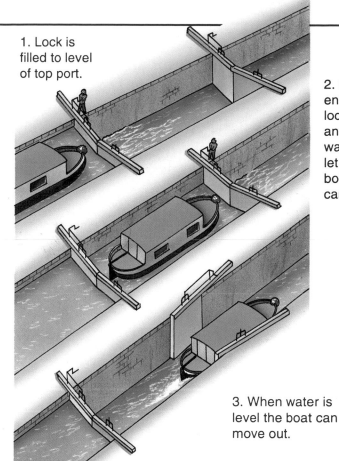

Kicking strap

Stern

Tiller

## Speedboat racing

Speedboat racing is the marine equivalent of motor racing. There are several formulas, each for boats of different size and power, and a series of races at different venues. Speedboats with one or more outboard motors race around circuits marked with buoys on rivers and in harbors. Most powerful are the Formula 1 boats which can reach speeds of over 100 mph.

## Luxury cruisers

At the top end of the leisure boat range is the luxury motor cruiser. These are the boats of the very rich. They have permanent crews, the latest technology, and no expense is spared on internal fittings. Many have garages for cars that the owners use when the boat is in port.

Luxury cruiser

# INNOVATIONS

Where there are boats, there will always be innovation, and a desire to design boats and ships that are faster, safer, more beautiful, cheaper to maintain, and more friendly to the environment. Today's hovercraft and hydrofoils would be unimaginable to designers of the early 1950s.
In the future, merchant ships are likely to become more streamlined and faster through the water, but their overall appearance will change little. Giant submarines may well carry freight underwater, and in naval circles there could be a revolution in design if development of stealth ships continues.

**Hovercraft**

The hovercraft (or air-cushion vehicle) was invented in 1955 by British engineer Sir Christopher Cockerell. The first "flight" was made in 1959 by an SRN1 hovercraft. A hovercraft is supported off the ground by a cushion of air. This is produced by large fans, and is held in place by a flexible skirt around the bottom of the craft. The great advantage of hovercraft over conventional boats is that there is no drag caused by a hull moving through the water. This means that even large hovercraft, such as the SR-N4, can travel at 75 mph.

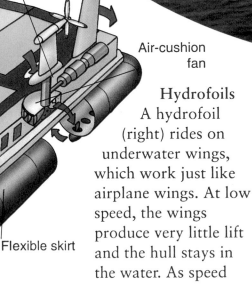

Passenger cabin

Gas turbine

Flight deck

Air-cushion fan

A hovercraft

Flexible skirt

**Hydrofoils**

A hydrofoil (right) rides on underwater wings, which work just like airplane wings. At low speed, the wings produce very little lift and the hull stays in the water. As speed increases, so the lift from the wings increases, and the hull begins to lift clear of the water riding on its wings or skis. This reduces the drag of the water on the hull, allowing it to reach much higher speeds.

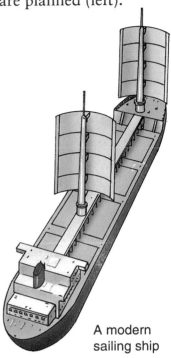

**Large liners**
One of the world's largest cruise ships, the Norwegian *Sovereign of the Seas*, completed in 1988, accommodates 2,282 passengers. There are ten passenger decks, swimming pools, lounges, and cinemas. Other even larger ships are planned (left).

**Return to sail?**
The high cost of fuel together with environmental consideration, led to various experiments with sail power. Several merchant ships were fitted with auxiliary sails so that engine power could be reduced when the wind was favorable. Computer-controlled vertical "wings" are also used.

A modern sailing ship

Air intake

Steering flap

Water-jet engine

**The future**
What lies in the future for the world of shipping? For merchant ships, efficiency is the key to success; so designers are always looking for more miles per ton of fuel, and crew size will be reduced by increased automation. High-tech developments are already taking place, such as the Japanese super conductive electro-magnet ship *Yamoto 1* (below) on her maiden voyage in Kobe Port, Japan.

# THE CAR

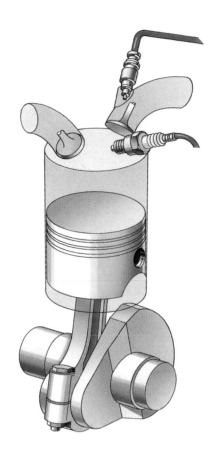

# CONTENTS

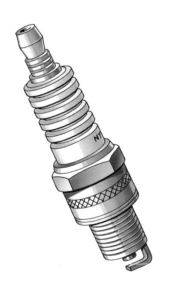

# THE CAR TODAY

Since the first cars chugged along cart tracks almost 100 years ago, everyday life has changed beyond recognition. The car has played a major role in that transformation. Today we can jump into the car and drive to school, to work, or to a vacation halfway across the continent. Freeways and expressways crisscross the land. We can travel as far in one day as the old horse-drawn carriages traveled in a month. This is the story of the car: how it was invented, how it developed over the years, and how it has affected so many aspects of our lives and our world.

## Too many cars?

Today traffic jams are a familiar sight in cities and on major roads all over the world. People waste time, and engines waste fuel. Many city centers are banning cars because of the noise, fumes, dirt, and traffic jams that cars cause. People are encouraged to use buses, trains, and bicycles, or to walk.

Police deal with traffic and cope with accidents

## Pollution problems

Car exhaust fumes are a major cause of air pollution. They shower particles onto the surroundings and contain chemicals that react with sunlight to form choking smog. They also add to acid rain and global warming.

## Eating up resources

Cars burn fuels made from petroleum (oil). They consume the world's limited supplies of petroleum at an amazing rate.

The car has transformed landscapes all over the world. Roads, parking lots, and roadside facilities take up more and more natural land. Gas stations must be sited at frequent intervals so that motorists do not run out of gas.

Car-making factories are major employers in many cities.

Leisure or shopping facilities will not attract customers unless people can drive and park there.

Service areas provide rest and food for travelers on long-distance journeys.

## Work and play
In the modern world the car is used for both work and leisure activities. On a vacation by car we can drive when and where we wish and visit interesting places. Driving to and from work or school each day is often a less pleasurable experience. Noise, fumes, and traffic lines can make it stressful and sometimes dangerous. Yet many people say they "have to" use the car. They insist there is no alternative.

## The modern car
The modern small car is a lightweight and efficient vehicle. It seats four or more people comfortably, and it is easy to handle in city centers or when cruising on the highway.

OUT

# PIONEERS OF THE CAR

The motor car evolved from the horse-drawn carriage. The first cars, from the early 1800s, looked like horse-pulled carts with engines attached – indeed, they were called "horseless carriages." For inventors, the key was to develop an engine that was powerful and reliable enough to propel a wheeled vehicle along roads that were often muddy cart tracks. Some inventors tried to use the steam engine and some steam-powered vehicles were used in Britain in the 1830s. Others worked on a new source of power, the internal combustion engine, fueled by gasoline or diesel fuel.

**Karl Benz**
During the 1880s, German engineer Karl Benz worked on internal combustion engines powered by coal gas, and then by gasoline. In 1885 he put one of these engines into a two-seater tricycle and created the first motorized cart, or motor car.

**Cugnot's cannon-puller** (above)
A French soldier, Nicholas-Joseph Cugnot, invented a three-wheeled steam tractor in about 1769. It was intended to replace horses for pulling army cannons. But when demonstrated before French generals, the tractor went out of control and the generals decided to keep their horses. In 1861 Canadian inventor Henry Seth Taylor attached a steam engine to a cart to form a steam carriage (above). Later steam was used to power cars, such as the Stanley Steamer. The steam engine was superseded by the internal combustion engine.

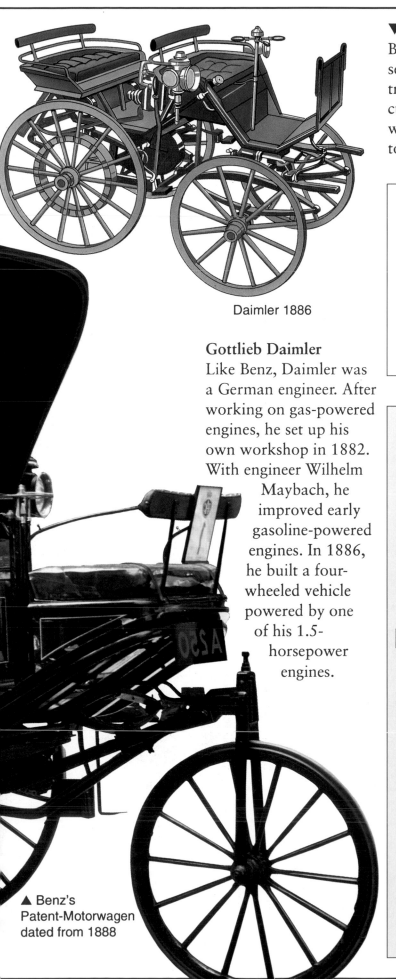

Daimler 1886

### Gottlieb Daimler

Like Benz, Daimler was a German engineer. After working on gas-powered engines, he set up his own workshop in 1882. With engineer Wilhelm Maybach, he improved early gasoline-powered engines. In 1886, he built a four-wheeled vehicle powered by one of his 1.5-horsepower engines.

▲ Benz's Patent-Motorwagen dated from 1888

### ▼ The Viktoria

By 1887, Karl Benz was selling motorized tricycles to the rich and curious. At first they were merely spluttering toys. But people soon realized that these strange new vehicles could be big business. Benz's Viktoria, which appeared in 1890, was the first car to be made in appreciable numbers.

### Motors and engines

The first practical internal combustion engine ran on gas and was invented by Belgian Etienne Lenoir in 1860. In 1876 German engineer Nicholas Otto improved it with the four-stroke cycle (see page 46). Daimler's early petrol engines ran at 900 rpm, much faster than the Otto engines. In the 1890s Rudolf Diesel invented the engine named after him (see page 47).

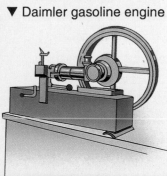

▲ Otto four- stroke engine

▼ Daimler gasoline engine

▼ Lenoir internal combustion gas engine

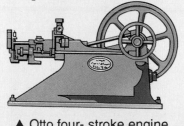

Diesel engine ▲

# THE FIRST MOTORISTS

After the experiments of the 1880s, the first car-making factories were set up in Germany and France during the 1890s. Engineers improved Daimler's engines, making them more powerful and reliable. Frenchman Emile Levassor was probably first to think of the car as a machine in its own right, and not just a cart without a horse. In 1891 he moved the engine from the back to the front, away from the mud and stones thrown up by the wheels. He also replaced the belt drive between engine and road wheels, with a clutch and a gearbox. The car as we know it today was quickly taking shape.

Napier 1913

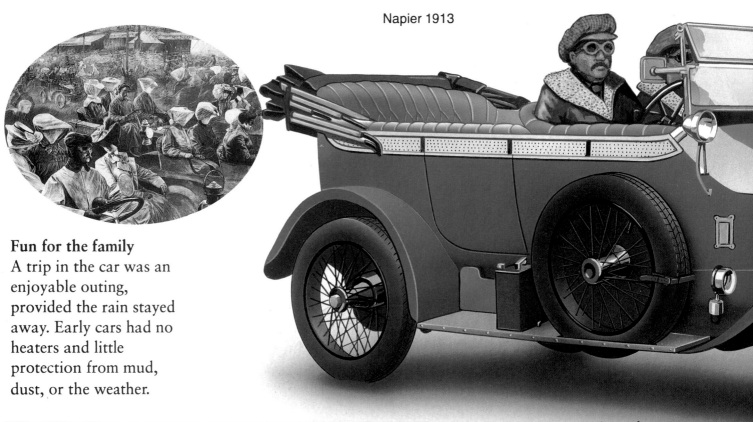

**Fun for the family**
A trip in the car was an enjoyable outing, provided the rain stayed away. Early cars had no heaters and little protection from mud, dust, or the weather.

**Roads to run on**
Cars were faster than horse-drawn carts, so they needed better roads. Instead of packed-down layers of earth and stone (top right), engineers devised smooth surfaces of tarmac or asphalt.

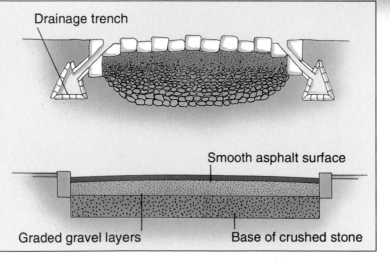

Drainage trench

Smooth asphalt surface

Graded gravel layers

Base of crushed stone

**A sign of status**
Big houses, fine furniture and beautiful horses had been signs of wealth for centuries. Around 1900 a new symbol of status appeared: the car. As yet, the car was not a useful means of transportation. Roads were muddy, rutted cart tracks, and refueling places were scarce.

### Flying the red flag

Under a law passed in Britain in 1865, steam traction engines were allowed to lumber along roads, provided they did not exceed 4 mph (6.5 kph) and a man with a red flag walked about 170 feet in front. The red flag was abandoned in 1878, but a footman still had to walk 60 feet in front. This law applied to any similar vehicle, including the first cars. In 1896 the footman was abandoned too, and the speed limit raised to almost 12 mph (20 kph).

Gas pump 1905

### Buying a car

At first, only the rich could afford a car. But many people gathered in car showrooms to gaze at these newfangled pieces of machinery, which seemed to have little practical use.

### Stopping for fuel

In the early days many car owners carried cans of spare fuel with them. There were no detailed maps and finding a gasoline station on a long journey was mostly a matter of luck.

### The maker's name

Car manufacturers were soon competing to produce the best, fastest, or cheapest vehicles. Companies such as Buick and Austin designed easily recognized nameplates.

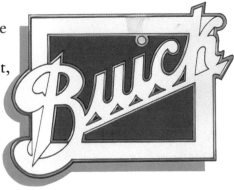

### Advertising

The growing car business involved designers, engineers, manufacturers, mechanics, and of course advertisers. As roads became busier, they became valuable places for posters, advertising the latest cars to drivers.

# CARS FOR EVERYONE

During the early 1900s, most cars became larger, more comfortable – and more costly. In America, however, entrepreneur Henry Ford was working in the other direction. Ford understood that there were only a limited number of rich people. His aim was to build small cars in huge numbers, so that they were cheap enough for the average person to buy. This would allow families to travel by car where they wanted. It was part of the freedom offered by the "American Dream", in which Ford believed so strongly. And the dream came true, with the Model T Ford.

◄ Model T, 1914

Ford production line, 1913

## The Model T
Production of the "Tin Lizzie" (so-called because the body was made of thin vanadium steel) began in 1908. The car had a four cylinder, three-liter, 20-horsepower engine, and a top speed of about 40 mph (65 kph). The Model T was designed to be inexpensive and long-lasting.

## Production line
Ford claimed that "the way to make automobiles is to make one automobile like another automobile, to make them all alike." At first the Model Ts were made on Ford's new invention, the production line, in his Detroit factory. In 1913 he introduced the moving assembly line, which has been copied around the world.

## Mass motoring

When the Model T ceased production in 1927, more than 15 million had been made. Cheap motoring meant more crowded roads. Without clear road markings and signs, driving was a hazardous business.

HOW MANY TUNES DOES IT PLAY, MISTER?

## "How many tunes does it play, mister?"

Cars in country areas were a source of bafflement. This postcard shows how the handcrank could be mistaken for the wind-up mechanism of a barrel organ!

## Car versus Horse (1904)

| | |
|---|---|
| Total cost over five years A pair of horses, including food, stabling, vet's bills : | $4,780 |
| Standard car, cost new: | $1,583 |
| gas and oil: | $760 |
| new set of tires: | $122 |
| wages for boy to clean and maintain: | $633 |
| repairs and spares: | $682 |
| minus resale price: | $487 |
| Total: | $3,293 |

## The cost of cars

Ford set the cost trend with the Model T, and the more that were made, the cheaper they became. A basic version cost $825 when it was introduced, and $260 some years later.

## Increasing choice

In the years before World War I, car manufacturers set up in most industrial countries. The home of mass production was America. European makers concentrated on the more expensive models built with hand tools, a development of the skilled tradition in building luxury horse-drawn carriages. Many famous names date from this period.

Peugeot 1905

Fiat 1914

Benz 1907

Mercedes 1914

# ENGINES AND TRANSMISSION

The heart of any car is its engine. Over the years different types of engines have come and gone, including steam engines, gas power, and electric motors. But gasoline and diesel engines power almost all modern vehicles. They are called internal combustion engines because the power comes from the burning (combusting) of fuel inside the cylinder. A steam engine is an external combustion engine, because the fuel is burned outside the engine, to heat water in the boiler.

In the four-stroke cycle the piston moves up and down twice, giving four movements, or strokes, for each explosion of gasoline inside the cylinder.

**The gasoline engine**
A modern gasoline engine is usually multi-cylindered. Inside each cylinder, a piston moves up and down as shown below. A system of cranks converts this up-and-down motion to the rotary motion of the crankshaft, which turns the gears in the gearbox, which turn the road wheels. Engine size or capacity is measured by the amount of air pushed out (displaced) from all the cylinders as the pistons move from their lowest to highest position. Today an average family car engine is about two liters.

▶ Modern twelve-cylinder five liter high performance BMW engine.

1. Induction or intake stroke – descending piston sucks in mixture of air and fuel.

2. Compression stroke – rising piston squeezes mixture of air and fuel vapor.

3. Ignition or power stroke – spark plug ignites mixture, which explodes and pushes piston down.

4. Exhaust stroke – rising piston pushes out exhaust gases.

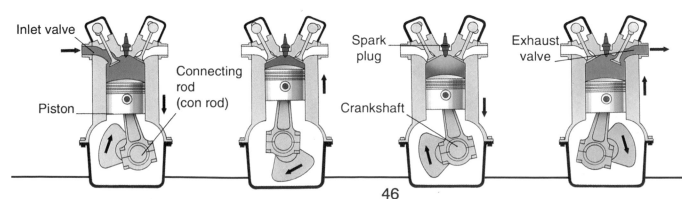

Inlet valve

Piston

Connecting rod (con rod)

Spark plug

Crankshaft

Exhaust valve

## Transmission

This part of the car transmits the engine's power to the road wheels. A system of gears in the gearbox, driven by the crankshaft, allows the engine to turn at its most effective speed for different road speeds. In manual transmission, the driver shifts gear.

The clutch pedal works levers that disconnect the crankshaft from the gears, so that gears can be shifted and the car can stay still when the engine is turning. In automatic transmission, introduced in 1937, the gears are shifted automatically.

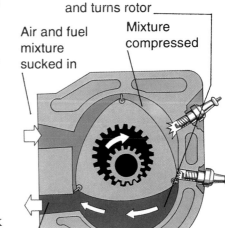

▲ Manual gear shift

▲ Automatic gearbox

### Wankel engine

This engine was developed by German scientist Felix Wankel in 1956. It produces rotary movement directly. A three-sided, off-center rotor turns in a specially shaped chamber. The air and fuel mixture is sucked in, compressed and ignited, and blown out in a cycle similar to the normal engine. Several engines may be used to power one car. Problems with the Wankel engine include rapid engine wear, excessive fuel consumption, and weak engine seals.

Mixture explodes and turns rotor

Air and fuel mixture sucked in

Mixture compressed

Burned gases blown out

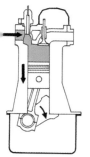

Induction

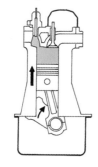

Compression

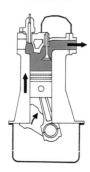

Ignition

Exhaust

### Diesel engine

A diesel engine does not have spark plugs. The air-fuel mixture is at high pressure, and becomes so hot that it ignites itself. Diesel engines last longer than gasoline engines and are becoming lighter and quieter.

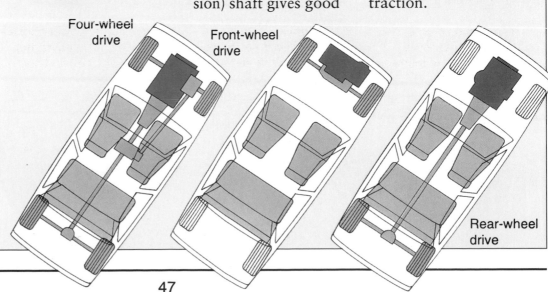

Peugeot front-wheel drive car

### Drive layouts

Since about 1900, most cars have had the engine at the front. Driving the two rear road wheels by a long propeller (transmission) shaft gives good weight distribution, stability and traction. Front wheel drive gives increased traction, but may alter the weight distribution. Four-wheel drive gives excellent traction.

Four-wheel drive

Front-wheel drive

Rear-wheel drive

# Fuel And Ignition

A car engine does not work unless its fuel is delivered in exactly the right amounts, at the right times, mixed with the right volume of air, so that it will burn. This is the job of the fuel and ignition systems. Several methods for mixing the air and fuel were developed, leading to the creation of the carburetor that could adjust the amounts of fuel and air according to the engine's speed and the load on it. As for ignition, the original Daimler engines had a platinum pipe in the top of the cylinder, which glowed red hot when heated by a burner at the other end, and ignited the fuel. Today electronic ignition systems and spark plugs do the job.

## Carburetors

Fuel will not burn without oxygen from the air. The carburetor draws fuel from the fuel tank and makes it into a very fine spray, which mixes with the correct amount of air.

Early carburetor, 1919 ▶

## Spark plugs

In a fast-running engine, each spark plug fires many times every second, to set fire to the fuel-air mixture inside the cylinder. The spark leaps across a gap at the tip of the plug, between the central electrode and the outer angled electrode. Up to 30,000 volts are needed to make each spark – far more than the usual 12-volt car battery can supply. The voltage is increased by a device called an ignition coil, using the principle of electrical induction.

## Distributor (left)

This feeds (distributes) high-voltage electricity to each spark plug at precisely the right moment, just as the piston below is compressing the fuel-air mixture. In many cars the distribution system is now electronic, controlled by a microchip.

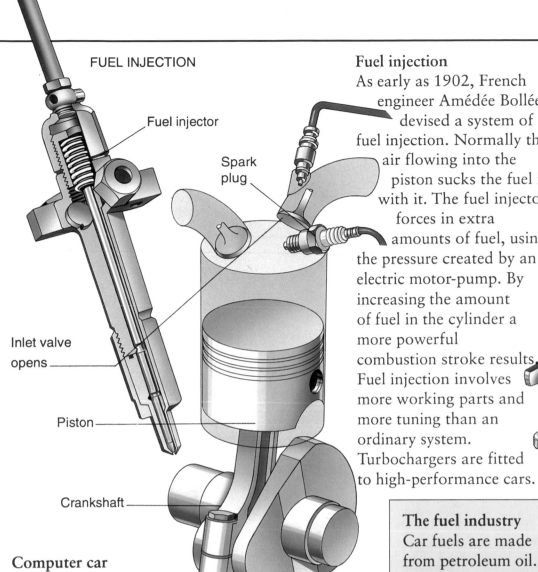

FUEL INJECTION

Fuel injector

Spark plug

Inlet valve opens

Piston

Crankshaft

## Fuel injection

As early as 1902, French engineer Amédée Bollée devised a system of fuel injection. Normally the air flowing into the piston sucks the fuel in with it. The fuel injector forces in extra amounts of fuel, using the pressure created by an electric motor-pump. By increasing the amount of fuel in the cylinder a more powerful combustion stroke results. Fuel injection involves more working parts and more tuning than an ordinary system. Turbochargers are fitted to high-performance cars.

## Turbo power

A turbocharger has a fan-shaped turbine blade that is turned by the exhaust gases (below). It compresses air so that more fuel can be forced into the cylinder.

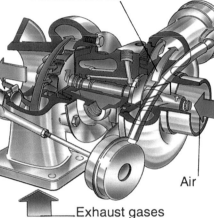

To the engine

Pressurized air

Air

Exhaust gases

## Computer car

Since 1966, when electronic fuel injection was developed, microchips have become more common in cars. They sense the load on the engine, monitor the air and fuel flow to the engine, and adjust the carburetor and fuel injection to give the best performance.

More recently, electronics can tell the driver about faults in the oil or hydraulic systems, brakes, tires, and even burned-out bulbs, as well as helping with route planning (above right).

A silicon chip

## The fuel industry

Car fuels are made from petroleum oil. So are jet fuels, engine lubricating oils, solvents, plastics, detergents, paints, tars, asphalts, and hundreds of other products. These substances are separated and purified from the dark, thick crude petroleum at giant oil refineries. The vast quantities of fuels used by cars, trucks, and other vehicles mean that the car and oil industries often work together to develop more efficient and cleaner fuels.

# CHASSIS, BRAKES, AND TIRES

The first cars had a framework or chassis built of wood and metal, as horse-pulled carriages did. As cars became faster and more powerful, the chassis had to be stronger in order to cope with the stresses. But fast driving over rutted roads was very uncomfortable. Suspension systems were invented, so that the road wheels could bounce over holes and bumps while the main body of the car stayed level. Air-filled tires made the ride smoother, and better brakes made it safer.

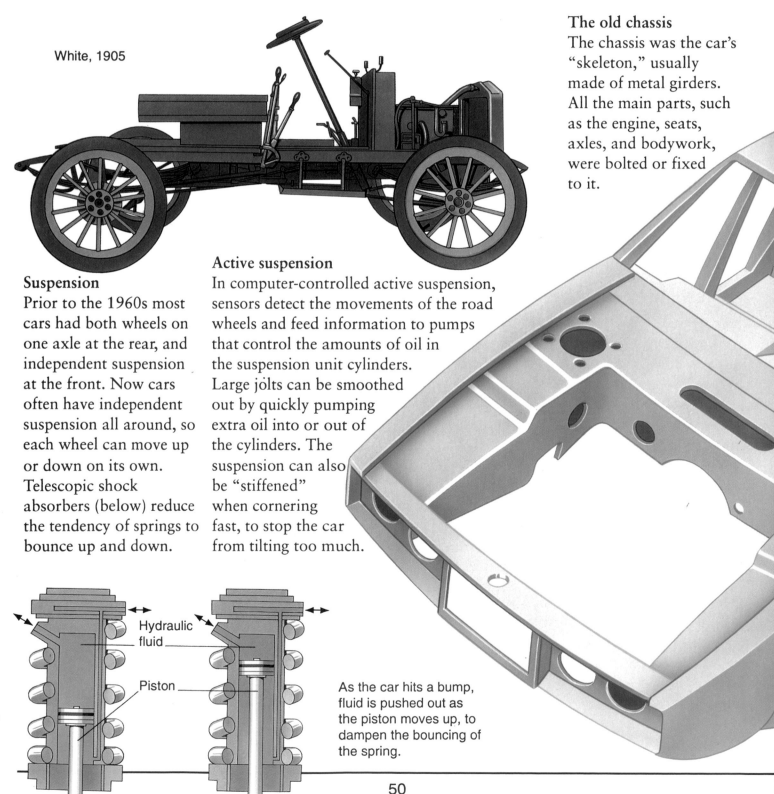

White, 1905

## The old chassis
The chassis was the car's "skeleton," usually made of metal girders. All the main parts, such as the engine, seats, axles, and bodywork, were bolted or fixed to it.

## Suspension
Prior to the 1960s most cars had both wheels on one axle at the rear, and independent suspension at the front. Now cars often have independent suspension all around, so each wheel can move up or down on its own. Telescopic shock absorbers (below) reduce the tendency of springs to bounce up and down.

## Active suspension
In computer-controlled active suspension, sensors detect the movements of the road wheels and feed information to pumps that control the amounts of oil in the suspension unit cylinders. Large jolts can be smoothed out by quickly pumping extra oil into or out of the cylinders. The suspension can also be "stiffened" when cornering fast, to stop the car from tilting too much.

Hydraulic fluid

Piston

As the car hits a bump, fluid is pushed out as the piston moves up, to dampen the bouncing of the spring.

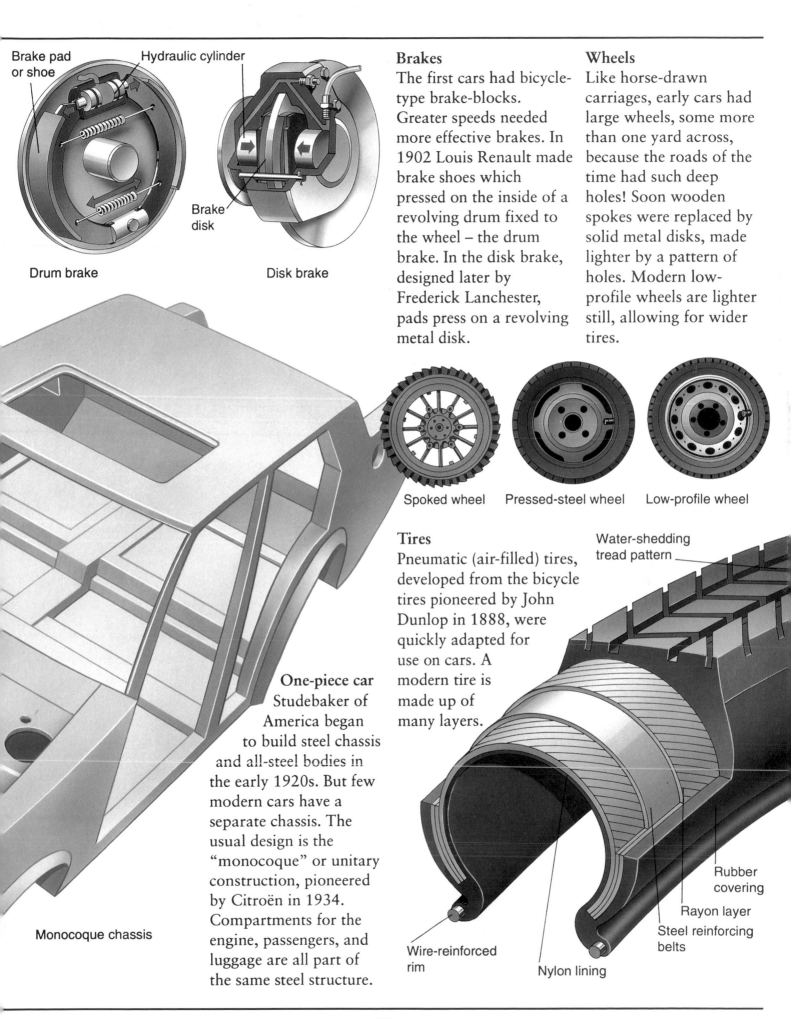

**Brake pad or shoe**

**Hydraulic cylinder**

**Brake disk**

Drum brake

Disk brake

## Brakes

The first cars had bicycle-type brake-blocks. Greater speeds needed more effective brakes. In 1902 Louis Renault made brake shoes which pressed on the inside of a revolving drum fixed to the wheel – the drum brake. In the disk brake, designed later by Frederick Lanchester, pads press on a revolving metal disk.

## Wheels

Like horse-drawn carriages, early cars had large wheels, some more than one yard across, because the roads of the time had such deep holes! Soon wooden spokes were replaced by solid metal disks, made lighter by a pattern of holes. Modern low-profile wheels are lighter still, allowing for wider tires.

Spoked wheel     Pressed-steel wheel     Low-profile wheel

## Tires

Pneumatic (air-filled) tires, developed from the bicycle tires pioneered by John Dunlop in 1888, were quickly adapted for use on cars. A modern tire is made up of many layers.

**Water-shedding tread pattern**

**Rubber covering**

**Rayon layer**

**Steel reinforcing belts**

**Nylon lining**

**Wire-reinforced rim**

**One-piece car**
Studebaker of America began to build steel chassis and all-steel bodies in the early 1920s. But few modern cars have a separate chassis. The usual design is the "monocoque" or unitary construction, pioneered by Citroën in 1934. Compartments for the engine, passengers, and luggage are all part of the same steel structure.

Monocoque chassis

# THE GOLDEN ERA

The two World Wars of 1914-18 and 1939-45 stimulated progress in many areas of science and engineering – including the car. After World War II, shortages of steel and gasoline meant a delay before the new models appeared. When they arrived, they were much more powerful and sleeker than their predecessors. As the shortages faded, a new generation of well-off teenagers was growing up in the major industrial countries. For them, cars were symbols of youth, style, and freedom.

**The gas-guzzlers**
During the 1950s, especially in America, cars became subjects of strange fashions. Cadillacs, Chevrolets, and Studebakers appeared in gaudy colors, and sprouted tail fins, grilles, and yards of shiny chrome plate. Their huge engines consumed large amounts of "gas" (gasoline or petrol), but the newly rich youngsters could easily afford it – at least, their parents could.

**The teen dream**
Young people of the 1950s and 60s rapidly adopted fast cars and motorcycles for their own generation. The difference between these powerful new machines and the old, slow cars reflected the generation gap between them and their parents.

Ford Thunderbird (T-bird) Coupé, 1956 ▶

**"Ridin' along in my automobile"**
Cars were a favorite subject of many pop songs by Chuck Berry (right), the Beach Boys, and others. Young people shook off the war memories and took to a new, relaxed life-style as they cruised along highways.

## The 1960s

The 1960s was the age of the small car. The German "Beetle" became immensely popular, and the British Mini's revolutionary design was partly a reaction to the huge cars of the 1950s. With front-wheel drive, and all-around rubber suspension, the Mini was fun to drive and easy to park. It was an instant success, and became a symbol of the fashionable "Swinging London."

Volkswagen Beetle launched in 1935

The Mini designed by Alec Issigonis in 1959

## Cars in daily life

By the 1960s, cars were no longer merely a means of transportation. They were an essential part of many events in daily life. New towns were designed with car-owners in mind. Drive-in cinemas, restaurants, banks, and even drive-in churches flourished. Parking lots took over great areas of land, so that workers could park near their factories and shoppers near their stores. The car was also a place where courting couples could be alone, and each town had its secluded "Lover's Lane."

## A place to park

The 1960s trend toward high-rise buildings affected cars, too. New methods of mixing and pouring concrete made possible the construction of multi-level garages. These were one solution to parking in city centers.

# IN-CAR ENTERTAINMENT

In the early years of cars, roads were small and narrow. They wound through towns and villages. Travelers enjoyed the countryside, stopped for rests and to visit places of interest, and broke long journeys by overnight stays. In the 1950s and 60s, freeways and expressways were built across the landscape, wide and straight. Drivers could cover hundreds of miles in a day. Along with the faster cars being developed, these roads opened up new possibilities for reaching faraway destinations on car trips. But there was a new problem: how to fill all those in-car hours.

## Style and comfort

A limousine is a large luxury car. It has deep, padded, reclining seats, and "extras" such as air conditioning. The stretch-limo has an extra section in the middle, making it even longer, so that passengers have plenty of leg room. These expensive cars are ideal for long journeys. They are quiet and comfortable, and often equipped with TV, phone, and even a cocktail bar.

A stretch-limo ▶

## Motown

In the 1920s many car makers set up in Detroit: Ford, General Motors, Packard, Hudson, Maxwell, and Dodge. In the 1960s a soul-based rhythmic music from Detroit became known as Motown, after the city's nickname, Motor Town. Diana Ross (left) was one of Motown's most famous stars

## Car phones

As the roads swell with more and more cars, so journey times are increasing, particularly in crowded areas. Mobile car phones allow motorists to be in contact with the office, family, and friends. The range of car phones can vary according to the type of system used, from local to international.

## In-car music

In 1922 the "father of radio" Guglielmo Marconi experimented with the British Daimler Company on car radios. Today's hi-fi multi-speaker car radio systems have come a long way since then. Other types of car music machines appeared as early as the 1900s. First came waxed cylinders, which rotated as a stylus (needle) played in the wavy groove in the wax. Next came vinyl record-players (phonograms), and cassettes. Modern cars are often fitted with Compact Disc (CD) players that use laser beams to read the microscopic humps and pits on the disc that encode the sounds.

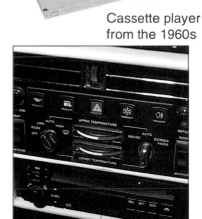

Cassette player from the 1960s

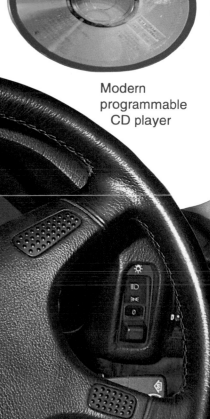

Modern programmable CD player

## At your fingertips

As early as 1929, car radios were being offered as extras by several American manufacturers. A modern family car bristles with gadgets (below). Most are within easy reach of the driver and operate by simple controls, so that he or she is not distracted. The radio, cassette tape, CD player, and computer are common fittings.

## Traffic information

Many radio stations (above) broadcast traffic news to give drivers advance warning of construction, accidents, and traffic tie-ups. These stations may gather their information from the police, spotter planes and helicopters, the patrols of road organizations, and drivers who phone in with up-to-the-minute details.

# COMFORT AND SAFETY

Sitting in the warmth of the latest family saloon, it is difficult for us to appreciate that the first cars were very drafty and uncomfortable, with leaky canvas roofs and no heating. Improvements have come gradually over the years, beginning with the first enclosed car in 1895, by makers Panhard. The windshield was offered as an "optional extra" in 1899, by manufacturers Dietrich-Bollée, and windshield wipers were first used by Cadillac in 1915. In recent years, safety in high-speed crashes has become an extremely important factor to consider when buying a car.

### Keeping warm

At one time, motorists would not dream of setting off without a warm coat and hat, gloves, and a travel rug for body and legs. An open car traveling at high speed could be a cold place, even on the sunniest days. The first car heaters took warmth from the engine exhaust, and were introduced in the United States in 1905. In 1926 heaters began to use warmth from the hot water in the engine's cooling system. Power-operated windows appeared in 1946, again in the U.S.

▶ In some modern cars, an air bag inflates to protect the driver in a crash.

### Air conditioning

The car air conditioning system cools air or warms it, humidifies (adds moisture) or dries it, and removes dust and smells, so that passengers remain comfortable. Air conditioning is useful in hot climates, especially when cars become stuck in long traffic jams. The benefit is not solely increased comfort. A motorist who becomes too hot and sticky may begin to drive less carefully.

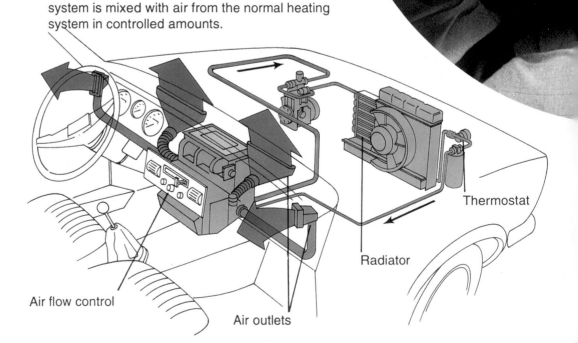

▼ Refrigerated air from a separate cooling system is mixed with air from the normal heating system in controlled amounts.

Thermostat

Radiator

Air flow control

Air outlets

## Testing

Every new type of car has to pass a long list of safety tests. Some involve crashing the car at high speed, to test the strength of the passenger section. Bumpers (fenders), brakes, lights, steering, fuel system, and traction are also checked, on the prototypes and then on selected samples from the production lines, before the car receives a certificate of roadworthiness.

## The safety cage

Today's cars usually have a stiffened "cage" around the passengers, with strengthening metal girders. Engine and luggage compartments form "crumple zones" that absorb the shock of a front or rear crash.

## Belting up

Seat belts first appeared in the 1920s. The modern seat belt adjusts and allows its wearer to move about in normal traveling. But if the car suddenly jerks, the belt locks to prevent the wearer from being hurled forward. Many countries now have laws enforcing the wearing of seat belts.

## Computer design

Nowadays, manufacturers depend heavily on computers. In CAD (Computer Aided Design), computer programs work out the streamlining of a particular design, how this affects fuel use, how much metal it would take to make the car body, and its strength in a crash.

# ECONOMY AND POLLUTION

Almost since Daimler and Benz put their pioneering vehicles on the market, there have been big, expensive cars and small, cheap ones. Most drivers bought the best they could afford. But the 1970s and 80s brought a new awareness. People began to understand about pollution and the need to preserve the countryside, and about conserving natural resources such as petroleum. The "green movement" spread, and the car was one of its main targets. Many people turned to smaller cars, which used less fuel and caused less pollution.

## Cleaning up the car

In 1940, there were about 50 million cars in the world. Today, there are more than 400 million, and the number is rising steadily. The noise, dust, smog, and smells caused by cars are a problem, especially in cities. In addition, car exhausts contain the gases carbon monoxide and carbon dioxide, which contribute to the environmental problem of global warming, and nitrous oxides, which cause acid rain. People have begun to demonstrate about the damage that millions of cars are doing to the environment. Some protests are even staged on bicycles (below). Car makers have responded by building smaller, more economical vehicles. Their ads emphasize engine efficiency, safety, less pollution, and streamlining, which looks good and increases fuel economy. Some new cars are designed so that metals and other materials can be recycled.

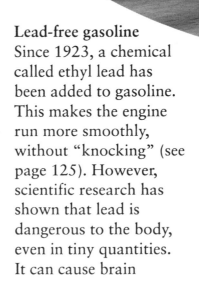

## Lead-free gasoline

Since 1923, a chemical called ethyl lead has been added to gasoline. This makes the engine run more smoothly, without "knocking" (see page 125). However, scientific research has shown that lead is dangerous to the body, even in tiny quantities. It can cause brain damage. People who breathe the dense lead fumes from car exhausts around busy roads may be at risk of mental and learning problems. So most countries now encourage motorists to buy cars that run on unleaded gasoline.

## Catalytic converters

A catalytic converter is fitted to a vehicle with an internal combustion engine. It is a special chamber in the exhaust pipe which filters out hazardous fumes from the engine, carrying out three chemical reactions to get rid of three main pollutants. A good catalytic converter cuts down emissions of nitrous oxides, the gases that help to make acid rain, by nine-tenths. Since 1981, catalytic converters have been required by law on new cars produced in the U.S. European countries are also introducing laws concerning catalytic converters.

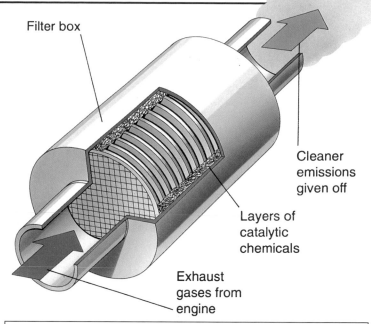

Filter box

Cleaner emissions given off

Layers of catalytic chemicals

Exhaust gases from engine

▼ A tiny Japanese "compact"

**Major manufacturers**
In 1950, the U.S. made two-thirds of the world's motor vehicles. By 1980 this share had gone down to about one-fifth. Japan had overtaken Britain, then Germany, and finally the U.S., to become the world's main vehicle-making country. This is partly due to the working methods in Japanese factories, and also to investment in automatic "robot" welders, assemblers, and painters.

## MOTOR VEHICLE PRODUCTION
in thousands of vehicles

|      | U.S. | Britain | France | Germany | Japan |
|------|------|---------|--------|---------|-------|
| 1930 | 2363 | 237     | 230    | 71      | 0.5   |
| 1950 | 8006 | 784     | 358    | 306     | 32    |
| 1970 | 8284 | 2098    | 2750   | 3842    | 5289  |
| 1980 | 8010 | 1313    | 3378   | 3878    | 11049 |
| 1990 | 9780 | 1566    | 3769   | 5148    | 13487 |

# THE ELECTRIC CAR

The electric car seems to solve many of today's car-caused problems. In an internal combustion engine, less than half the energy in the fuel is converted into useful energy, to power the car. In an electric motor, this figure is nine-tenths. Electric cars are quiet, efficient, and give off no poisonous fumes. So why don't we all use them? There are various reasons, particularly the limitations of the batteries, which need to be recharged frequently. People who are used to the convenience of a gasoline or diesel engine would find an electric car restricting for this reason.

## A century of electric cars

The electric car is not a new idea. Powerful electric motors and batteries were developed late in the last century.

By 1900, several electric cars were available to the public. Henry Ford considered electric motors and also gas engines for his cars, before deciding on internal combustion.

Modern prototype electric car

## The Hybrid

This is both electric and gasoline-driven – a hybrid. Its batteries can usually be kept fully charged from the mains. On long journeys, a small engine drives a generator that makes enough electricity to keep the batteries charged. Individual electric motors drive each road wheel. Since the shafts of the motors turn powerfully at low speeds, this type of car needs no gears.

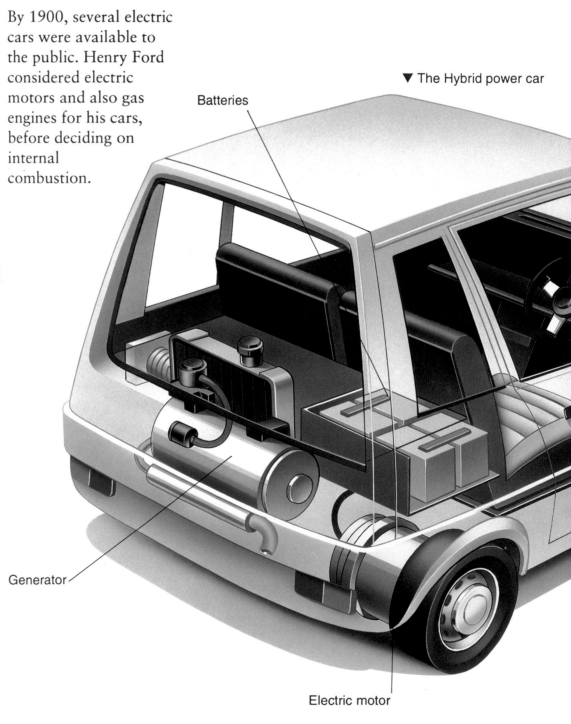

▼ The Hybrid power car

Batteries

Generator

Electric motor

## Better batteries

Normally batteries in an electric car restrict journeys to about 120 miles. If the batteries have to be recharged, the vehicle is out of action. Battery technology is advancing, with the development of rechargeable NiCad (Nickel-Cadmium), Lithium, and other fuel cells (right), but progress is steady rather than spectacular. A break-through in the next few years looks unlikely. One solution would be to make battery-changing centers as common as gasoline stations.

**Electric motor**

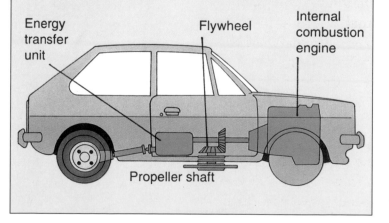

## Electric vehicles

Electrically powered vehicles are a familiar sight as golf carts and small carts used in large shopping centers. These vehicles travel relatively short distances, and their electric motors cope efficiently with constant stopping and starting. The drivers can return to base and pick up a freshly charged vehicle when necessary.

## The electric trike

The Sinclair C5 was launched in 1985. It had a small electric motor and was assisted by pedal-power from the driver. But it was slow and vulnerable in traffic.

## Other energy sources

Today's cars could be improved by using the internal combustion engine more efficiently. As a car brakes, energy is lost as heat in the brake drums or disks. One idea is to transfer the energy of the slowing car to a heavy flywheel, making it spin faster as the car slows. This energy could then be "recycled" back to the road wheels as the car accelerates again (below). Another idea is to use renewable fuels, obtained from plants such as oilseed-rape or sugar cane.

Energy transfer unit

Flywheel

Internal combustion engine

Propeller shaft

▲ Sinclair C5

# THE FUTURE

Karl Benz and Gottlieb Daimler would be amazed, and perhaps horrified, to see the way their inventions have affected the world. What lies in the future? Cars give us so much personal freedom, to go where and when we wish, that people are unlikely to choose to give them up. Unless public transportation improves massively, it cannot offer an alternative, especially for those in rural areas. One way forward may be to make cars simpler and more efficient, so that we can enjoy our freedom, while needing to worry less about polluting and destroying our world.

## More cars

Car use is rocketing. About 70 new cars drive onto the world's roads *every minute*. In the United States, the number of cars more than doubled between 1960 and 1990. No sooner is a large new roadway completed, than it is filled bumper-to-bumper. Governments agree that cars create pollution problems, and consume natural resources. But moves to restrict car use would be unpopular. A government that introduced such measures would be unlikely to be re-elected.

## Third World demand

As Third World countries develop, car use rises dramatically. If there were as many cars in Third World countries as there are in the West, the effect on the environment would be catastrophic. But developing countries have as much right to cars as western countries.

## The future – now?

Tomorrow's cars will probably be made from lightweight, corrosion-proof materials, such as special plastics and metal alloys. They will be even sleeker, to cut down wind resistance and to increase fuel economy. Cars like the electric Renault Zoom (left) may contract to make parking easy.

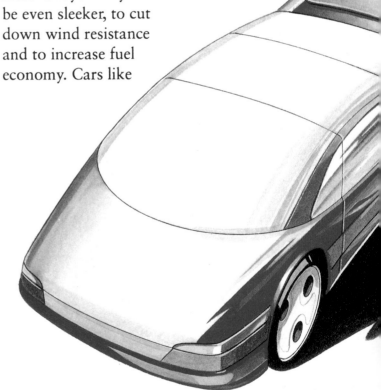

▲ The car of the future?

## Predicting the future

In years gone by, experts predicted all kinds of amazing advances in the car. One common idea was that cars would lose their road wheels and be able to counteract gravity, and so "float" above the ground like mini-hovercraft. Some predictions, such as greater streamlining and more use of plastics, have come true. However, the basic gasoline engine, steering wheel, gears, and four road wheels still remain.

▶ 1960s prediction

▼ 1980s prediction

▼ 1990s electric car

### Action against pollution

Traffic fumes and smog are so bad in some cities that they are a public health hazard. Los Angeles has identified electric vehicles as one way to reduce the problem. It intends to have one-tenth of vehicles running on electricity by the year 2000.

### Making cars

Car factories are becoming more automated. Computers and robots carry out the tedious jobs of assembling cars, piece by piece, accurately and tirelessly (see below). But there will probably always be a small demand for special cars, hand-made to meet customers' requirements.

### Fuels of the future

If we continue to burn gasoline, diesel, and other petroleum-based fuels at today's rates, the petroleum still in the ground will run out in 50-100 years. Can we improve engine efficiency? Yes. Most cars travel about 18-20 miles per gallon of fuel. Test cars being developed now can run over 60 miles per gallon. Another possibility is solar power – using the energy in sunlight to make electricity for electric cars. In 1987 the experimental car Sunraycer crossed Australia using solar power generated by solar panels, as in the prototype pictured below.

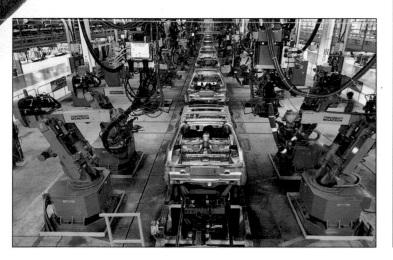

# The Book of GREAT INVENTIONS

# FLYING
## MACHINES

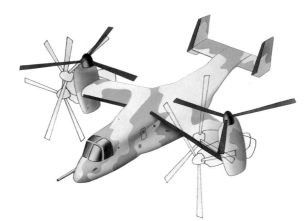

# CONTENTS

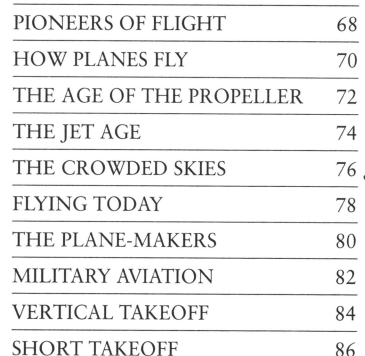

# THE INVENTION OF FLIGHT

Flight has been one of the great technical challenges of the 20th century. The first powered flight was achieved less than a hundred years ago. Today we can fly to the other side of the world in less than a day. Aircraft are a common sight in the sky, from jetliners carrying vacationers and business travelers, to fighter planes in an air display, or helicopters on a rescue mission. This is the story of the invention of the flying machine, and of the developments in technology that have resulted in the aircraft of today. It is also the story of the benefits and problems that aircraft have brought to the modern world.

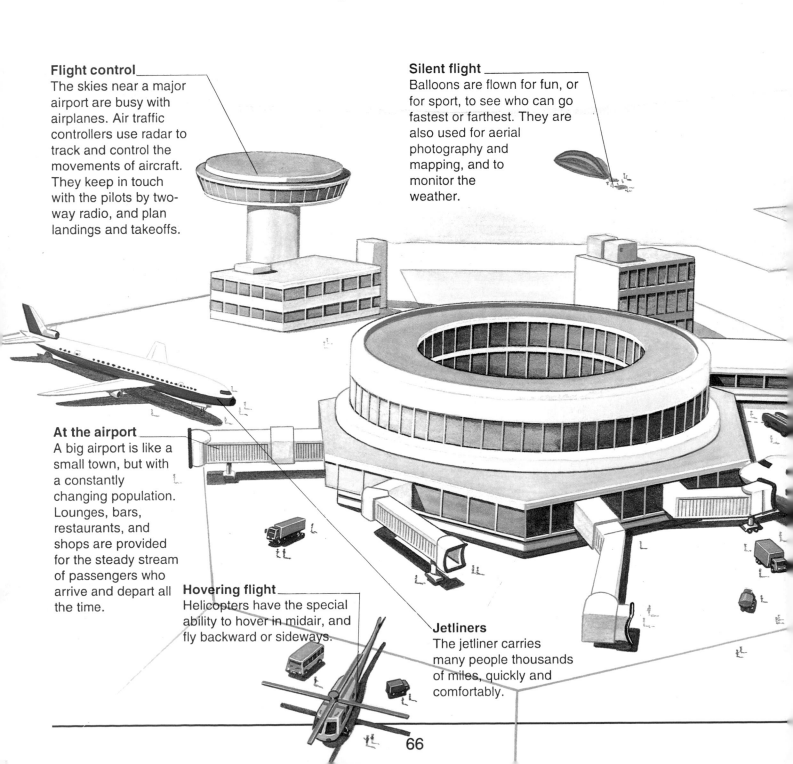

**Flight control**
The skies near a major airport are busy with airplanes. Air traffic controllers use radar to track and control the movements of aircraft. They keep in touch with the pilots by two-way radio, and plan landings and takeoffs.

**Silent flight**
Balloons are flown for fun, or for sport, to see who can go fastest or farthest. They are also used for aerial photography and mapping, and to monitor the weather.

**At the airport**
A big airport is like a small town, but with a constantly changing population. Lounges, bars, restaurants, and shops are provided for the steady stream of passengers who arrive and depart all the time.

**Hovering flight**
Helicopters have the special ability to hover in midair, and fly backward or sideways.

**Jetliners**
The jetliner carries many people thousands of miles, quickly and comfortably.

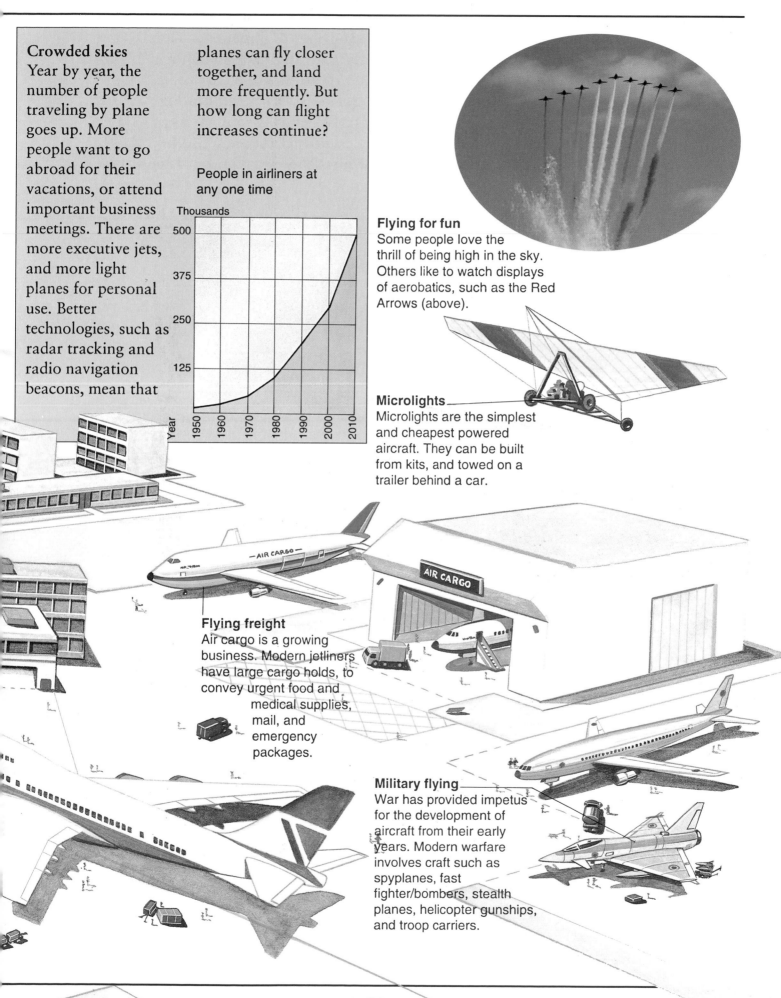

**Crowded skies**

Year by year, the number of people traveling by plane goes up. More people want to go abroad for their vacations, or attend important business meetings. There are more executive jets, and more light planes for personal use. Better technologies, such as radar tracking and radio navigation beacons, mean that planes can fly closer together, and land more frequently. But how long can flight increases continue?

People in airliners at any one time

**Flying for fun**
Some people love the thrill of being high in the sky. Others like to watch displays of aerobatics, such as the Red Arrows (above).

**Microlights**
Microlights are the simplest and cheapest powered aircraft. They can be built from kits, and towed on a trailer behind a car.

**Flying freight**
Air cargo is a growing business. Modern jetliners have large cargo holds, to convey urgent food and medical supplies, mail, and emergency packages.

**Military flying**
War has provided impetus for the development of aircraft from their early years. Modern warfare involves craft such as spyplanes, fast fighter/bombers, stealth planes, helicopter gunships, and troop carriers.

# PIONEERS OF FLIGHT

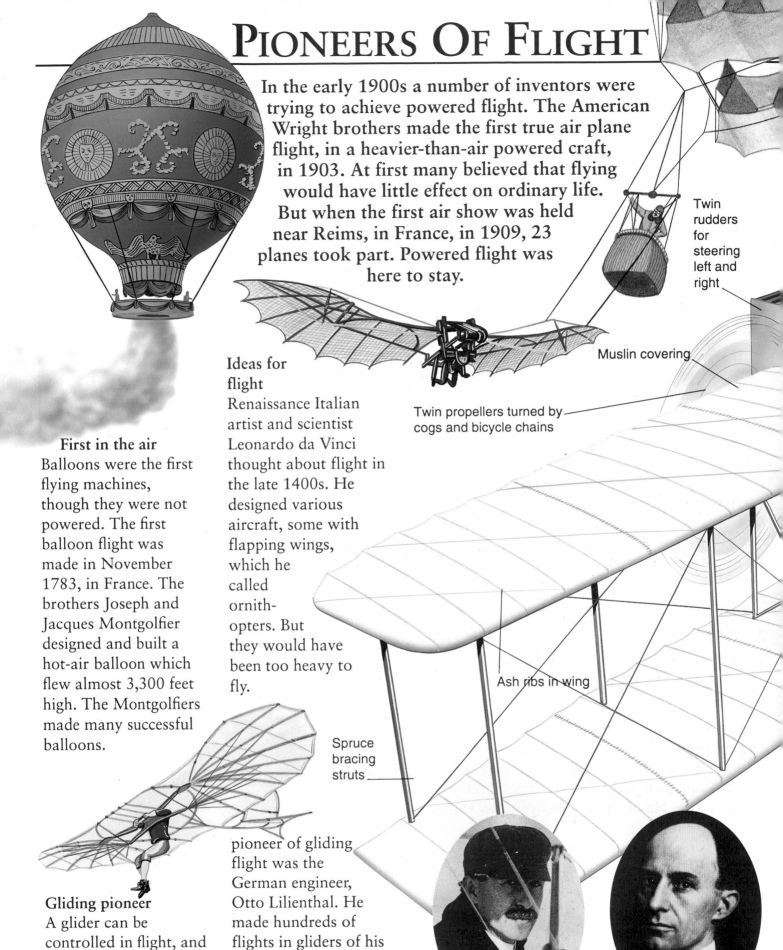

In the early 1900s a number of inventors were trying to achieve powered flight. The American Wright brothers made the first true air plane flight, in a heavier-than-air powered craft, in 1903. At first many believed that flying would have little effect on ordinary life. But when the first air show was held near Reims, in France, in 1909, 23 planes took part. Powered flight was here to stay.

Twin rudders for steering left and right

Muslin covering

Twin propellers turned by cogs and bicycle chains

Ash ribs in wing

Spruce bracing struts

**First in the air**
Balloons were the first flying machines, though they were not powered. The first balloon flight was made in November 1783, in France. The brothers Joseph and Jacques Montgolfier designed and built a hot-air balloon which flew almost 3,300 feet high. The Montgolfiers made many successful balloons.

**Ideas for flight**
Renaissance Italian artist and scientist Leonardo da Vinci thought about flight in the late 1400s. He designed various aircraft, some with flapping wings, which he called ornith-opters. But they would have been too heavy to fly.

**Gliding pioneer**
A glider can be controlled in flight, and uses up-currents of air to go higher, but has no engine. The chief pioneer of gliding flight was the German engineer, Otto Lilienthal. He made hundreds of flights in gliders of his own design, in the 1890s. He crashed and died in 1896.

Orville Wright

Wilbur Wright

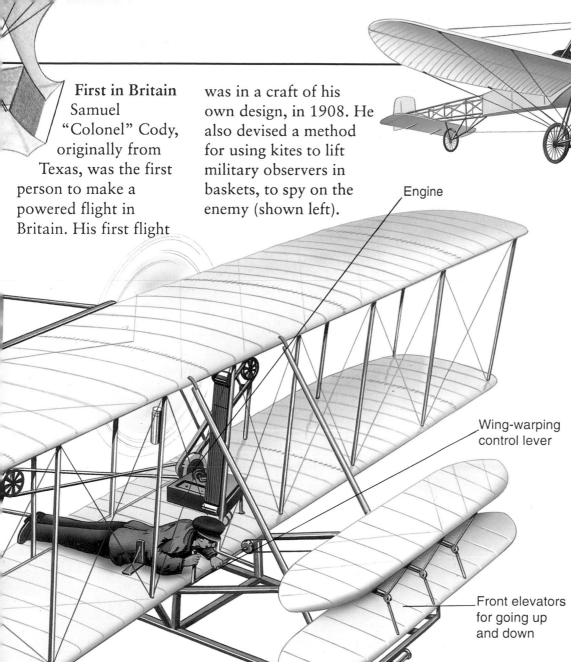

## First in Britain

Samuel "Colonel" Cody, originally from Texas, was the first person to make a powered flight in Britain. His first flight was in a craft of his own design, in 1908. He also devised a method for using kites to lift military observers in baskets, to spy on the enemy (shown left).

Engine

Wing-warping control lever

Front elevators for going up and down

Wright *Flyer*

Biplane (double-winged) design

## Across The Channel

After the Wrights' pioneering efforts, the London *Daily Mail* newspaper offered a prize of £1,000 for the first plane flight across The Channel between England and France. The winner was Frenchman Louis Blériot. He made the crossing on July 25, 1909, in his tiny plane *Blériot No XI* (above).

## Across the Atlantic

During World War I, aircraft developed greatly. The challenge after the war was to fly across the Atlantic. John Alcock and Arthur Brown did this in June 1919, in a converted *Vickers Vimy* bomber.

## First plane flight

The age of the plane began on a cold morning in December 1903, at Kitty Hawk in North Carolina. Orville Wright flew about 120 feet in 12 seconds, at 7-10 feet high, in the *Flyer*, designed and built with his brother Wilbur. The Wright brothers ran a bicycle business in Dayton, Ohio, which provided the money for their flying experiments. The key to their success was a lightweight, four-cylinder petrol engine. Although some early pioneers had experimented with steam-powered engines, only the internal combustion engine proved compact, yet powerful enough to propel a plane through the air.

Route of Alcock and Brown

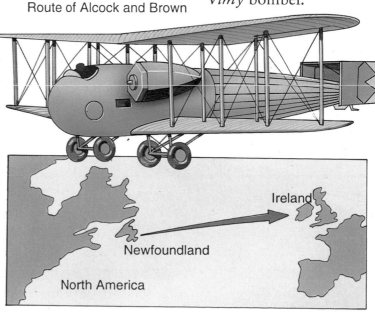

Ireland

Newfoundland

North America

# HOW PLANES FLY

Although the size, shape, and engine layout of aircraft has changed over the years, most of today's planes have the same basic components. There is a central tube, the fuselage, to which the wings, tail plane, and landing gear are attached. The fuselage of a jetliner is usually made of sections of metal. It may be pressurized to provide breathable air at high altitudes. Most aircraft have the basic design shown here.

Elevator

Tail plane (two small wings

Rudder

The fin provides stability.

## Staying in the air

The engine propels the plane forward, but its wings keep it in the air. Seen from the side, the wing has a curved shape, the airfoil section. Air flows faster over the more-curved upper surface. This creates lower air pressure above and higher air pressure below, and so the wing is "sucked" upward by a force called lift. Moveable surfaces on the wings , the slats, flaps, and spoilers, create more lift for takeoff, or smoother streamlining for high-speed cruising.

## Control surfaces

A typical plane controls its direction through the air by three main types of control surfaces. These are the rudder (shown in green here), elevators (purple), and ailerons (orange). They are moved into the airstream rushing past, to twist or push the plane in a certain direction, as explained on the right. The control surfaces are moved by cables running around pulleys, which are linked to the pilot's controls. The control column (joystick) works the elevators and ailerons. The rudder pedals operate the rudder. In some larger aircraft the controls have hydraulic pumps or electric motors to assist movements.

Aileron

LIFT

Faster air flow

Slower air flow

## Wing-warping

Early airplanes such as the *Flyer* were controlled partly by wing-warping. Wires pulled on the ends of the flimsy, flexible wings and twisted them slightly out of shape, making the plane bank (turn).

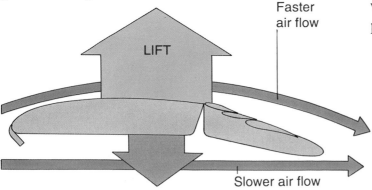

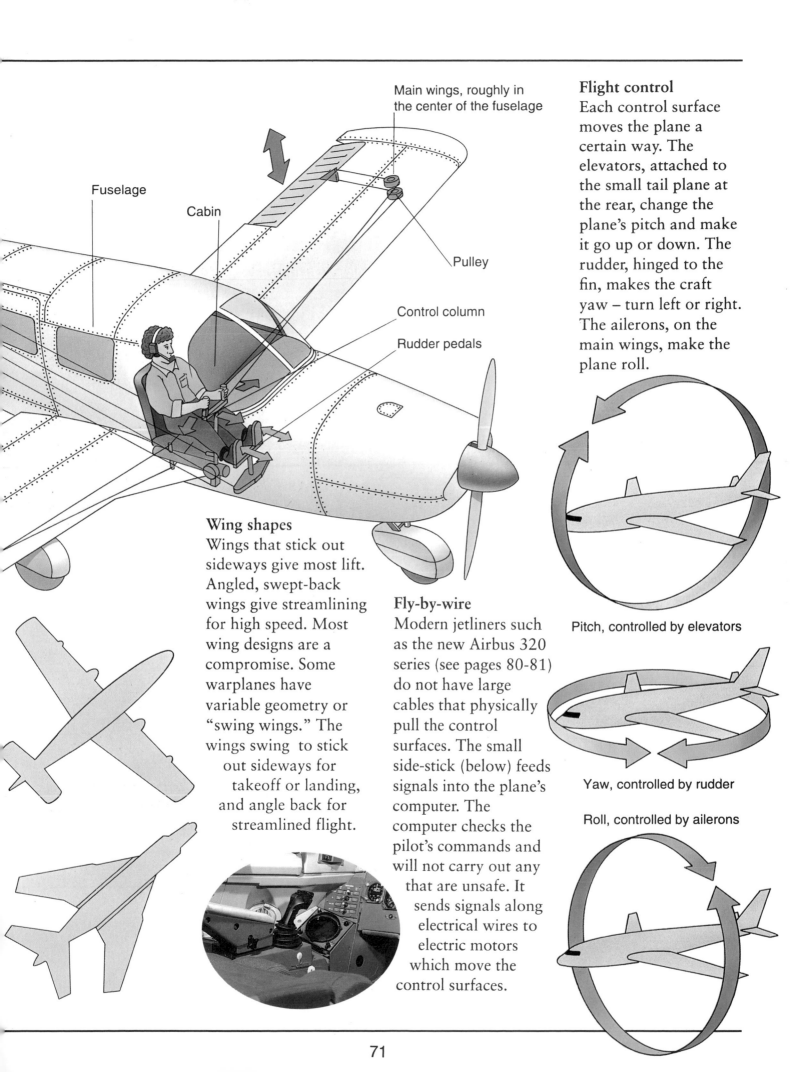

Main wings, roughly in the center of the fuselage

Fuselage

Cabin

Pulley

Control column

Rudder pedals

## Flight control

Each control surface moves the plane a certain way. The elevators, attached to the small tail plane at the rear, change the plane's pitch and make it go up or down. The rudder, hinged to the fin, makes the craft yaw – turn left or right. The ailerons, on the main wings, make the plane roll.

Pitch, controlled by elevators

Yaw, controlled by rudder

Roll, controlled by ailerons

## Wing shapes

Wings that stick out sideways give most lift. Angled, swept-back wings give streamlining for high speed. Most wing designs are a compromise. Some warplanes have variable geometry or "swing wings." The wings swing to stick out sideways for takeoff or landing, and angle back for streamlined flight.

## Fly-by-wire

Modern jetliners such as the new Airbus 320 series (see pages 80-81) do not have large cables that physically pull the control surfaces. The small side-stick (below) feeds signals into the plane's computer. The computer checks the pilot's commands and will not carry out any that are unsafe. It sends signals along electrical wires to electric motors which move the control surfaces.

# THE AGE OF THE PROPELLER

Only a dozen years after the first powered flight, war planes were in action in World War I. They were used first for reconnaissance, and later as fighters and bombers. During the course of the war, airplanes developed from flimsy, open-air machines to highly maneuverable craft which provided good protection for the aviator. Their engines became powerful and reliable. After the war this technology was put to civilian use. The first airliners were built from bomber planes, but soon purpose-designed airliners were being made.

## Propeller power

The first planes were powered by propellers. A "prop" spins around very fast and pushes air back, pulling the plane forward. Early plane propellers were driven by lightweight piston engines, adapted from car or motorcycle engines. Soon engines were being specially designed for planes. The "rotary" engine was invented in 1909. Its cylinders were arranged in a circle around the central crankshaft. They rotated with the propeller while the crank stayed still. This solved the problem of keeping the engine cool, while the power generated was greatly increased.

Graf Zeppelin

## Flying boats and airships

Flying boats like the Boeing 314 Clipper offered greater comfort to passengers. Even more luxurious were the vast airships of the Zeppelin company, but their life was short. A series of disasters culminated in the destruction of the *Hindenberg* in 1937, when 36 people died. This spelt the end of the airship era.

## Interwar years

No sooner had the war ended than the first airlines were set up to carry fee-paying passengers. Britain's Imperial Airways launched their first service to Paris in 1924, and United Air Lines their flights between Chicago and San Francisco in 1934.

Boeing 314 Clipper

Viewing deck

Ford Trimotor

## The "Tin Goose"

The first passenger planes were noisy and cold. A new era of air transport was begun by the Ford Trimotor, one of the first planes built specifically to carry passengers. The "Tin Goose" had a passenger cabin constructed of thin metal plates fixed to a metal frame. It revolutionized aircraft design, and with its successors, the Boeing 247 and the Douglas DC-2, was the forerunner of today's airliners.

Douglas
DC-3 Dakota

The boat-shaped hull of the flying boat allowed it to land and take off on a lake or sea. At the time there were few airports with long hard-surfaced runways.

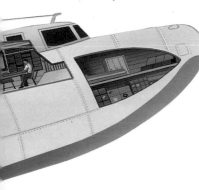

## From Supermarine to Spitfire

Advances made in air technology during the interwar years were taken up by the military when World War II broke out. The technology behind the Supermarine seaplane, designed for speed-racing, was used in the development of the Spitfire fighter plane, so famous during World War II.

## Postwar years

World War II saw an endless quest for ever-faster fighters, longer-range bombers, and increasingly sophisticated technology. The development of radar (see page 76) meant that aircraft could be "seen" at night. When the war ended, aircraft designed as warplanes were adapted for civilian use. The Douglas DC-3 Dakota, the most successful commercial airplane of all time, developed from the DC-1 and DC-2. Many are still in service around the world. The Boeing Stratocruiser was a direct descendant of the B29 bomber. It set new standards for trans-Atlantic flights.

Vickers-Supermarine
Spitfire

# THE JET AGE

In World War II, fast fighters such as the Spitfire, the Messerschmitt 109, and Mustang continued the development of warplane technology. But air forces wanted even greater speed to outfly the enemy, and there is a limit to the speed at which propeller-driven aircraft can fly. The result was the jet engine. Although jet fighters took part in combat, they arrived too late to have a great effect on the war's outcome. But by the 1950s, jet-powered planes were in regular service.

**The first jets**

Jet engines were developed in the 1930s, in England by Frank Whittle and his team, and in Germany by Hans von Ohain and his team. The first jet plane to fly was a German test version, the Heinkel He 178, in August 1939. The Gloster Whittle was another early jet plane, powered by one of Whittle's engines. The first jet plane to enter military service was the RAF's Gloster Meteor, in July 1944.

**Jets in combat**

The first jets to fly into combat were German Messerschmitt Me 262's, in September 1944. They startled enemy pilots by their top speed of over 500 mph (800 km/h), and by their lack of propellers!

**The developing jet**

In the years following World War II, aero-engineers searched for new metals and alloys. It was essential that these could withstand the enormous temperatures inside the jet engine, and the heat caused by great friction when flying through the air at such tremendous speed.

Exhaust thrust

Combustion chamber

Bypass ducts

The North American F-86 Super Sabre was the first faster-than-sound jet fighter to go into regular service, from 1954.

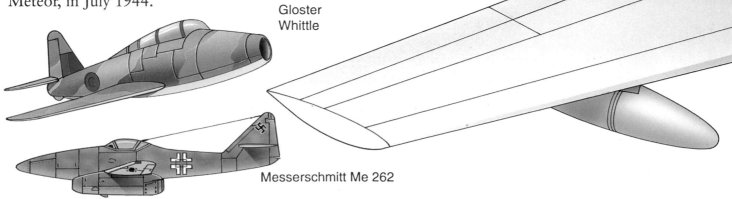

Gloster Whittle

Messerschmitt Me 262

## How the jet works

A gas turbine or turbojet draws in air, compresses (squashes) it, mixes it with fuel, and sets fire to it in a type of continuous explosion. The heated air expands, and forces its way out of the exhaust pipe, creating the "jet" of hot gases that gives the engine its nickname.

There are several types of jet design. Most modern jetliners are powered by turbofan engines, shown below. The engine gets its name from the huge fan-shaped turbine at the front. This blows air around the main engine, and also sucks air inside the engine, where a set of smaller turbines spin around rapidly to compress it. The compressor is driven by another set of turbines in the exhaust system, which is turned by the hot gases blasting out of the back.

### The sound barrier

Today's jets regularly fly faster than sound. In the 1940s, many people thought that flying faster than sound was impossible. As planes approached that speed, they were buffeted by powerful shock waves. Charles "Chuck" Yeager first broke the sound barrier safely on October 14, 1947, in the Bell X-1 rocket plane (above).

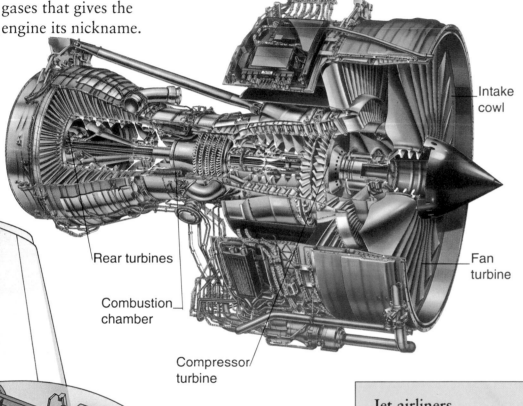

Intake cowl

Rear turbines

Combustion chamber

Compressor turbine

Fan turbine

Jet air intake

Nose intake

### Jet airliners

The first jet-powered passenger plane was the British de Havilland Comet, below, test-flown in 1949, and in regular service by 1952. It was eventually overtaken in numbers of planes by the U.S. Boeing 707.

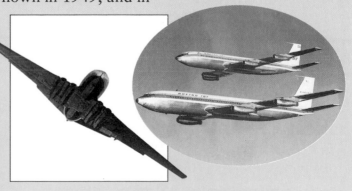

75

# THE CROWDED SKIES

The first pilots carried a few maps, an accurate timepiece, and a magnetic compass to help them navigate. Our skies are now hundreds of times busier, with planes flying ten times faster. Air Traffic Control (ATC) has become increasingly sophisticated. Before each flight the crew are given a detailed flight plan. ATC gives permission for takeoff, and clears the plane's flight through international air lanes to its destination.

Borrowed from boats Pioneer aviators navigated with the help of star charts and the sextant, left.

This measures the angle between the horizon and the Sun, Moon, star, or planet.

**A great invention** Radar means RAdio Detection And Ranging. Like many inventions, radar was developed in war time, in this case, during World War II. A radar transmitter sends out radio signals, and the receiver picks up echoes that bounce back from any objects in range. Each "blip" on a radar screen represents and aircraft. The picture shows British radar operators in the 1960s.

1 Weather radar
2 ILS Localizer receiver
3 ILS Glidescope receiver
4 VHF communications aerial
5 Satellite communications aerial

6 Radio altimeters
7 Omega aerial
8 VOR receiver
9 Avionics bay

### On-board navigation
Once airborne, it is vital for pilots to know exactly where they are. Planes possess many navigation systems, above, and the technology of navigation improves almost monthly. Radio signals are transmitted by special ground-based radio beacons, or by aircraft themselves, to aid navigation. Plane radar receivers can show the bearing, or direction, that the radio signals come from. The aircraft's transponders transmit a positive identification signal and a height reading.

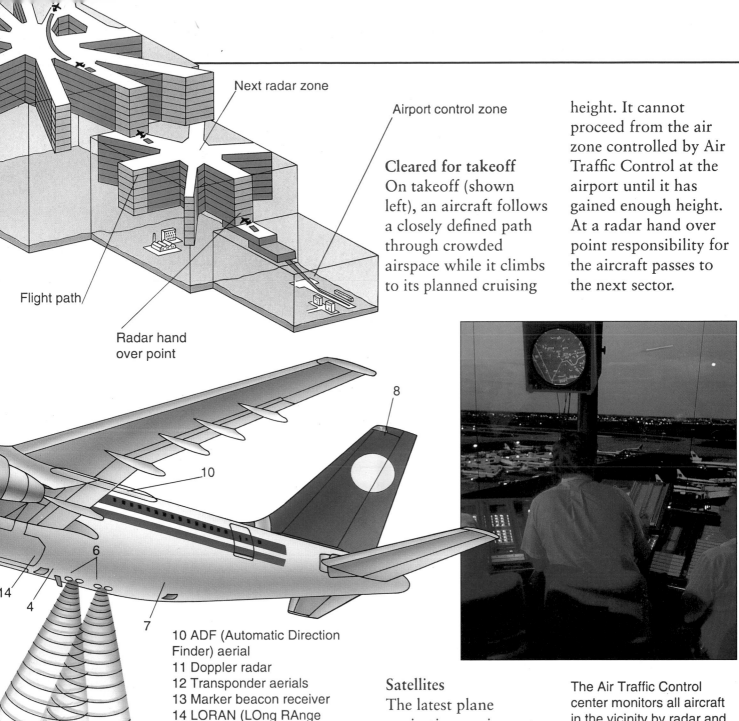

Next radar zone

Airport control zone

Flight path

Radar hand over point

### Cleared for takeoff

On takeoff (shown left), an aircraft follows a closely defined path through crowded airspace while it climbs to its planned cruising height. It cannot proceed from the air zone controlled by Air Traffic Control at the airport until it has gained enough height. At a radar hand over point responsibility for the aircraft passes to the next sector.

8

10

6

14

4

7

10 ADF (Automatic Direction Finder) aerial
11 Doppler radar
12 Transponder aerials
13 Marker beacon receiver
14 LORAN (LOng RAnge Navigation aerial
15 DME (Distance Measuring Equipment) aerials

The Air Traffic Control center monitors all aircraft in the vicinity by radar and radio, and clears them for landing and takeoff.

### Satellites

The latest plane navigation equipment receives signals from below, and also above, from satellites orbiting the Earth. The NAVSTAR navigation system provides signals from at least four satellites at any one time. The in-flight navigation computer calculates the craft's position at any one instant to the nearest 300 feet.

### Flight paths

The skies around a major airport are divided into pathways and corridors, marked by VOR (Very high-frequency Omni-directional Range) beacons. While a plane waits to land it queues, or "stacks", circling around and around at a certain height over a beacon in the vicinity. When instructed by ATC, it proceeds to the next lowest level, and ultimately to a stack near the airport itself. Finally, it is given the all clear for final approach and landing.

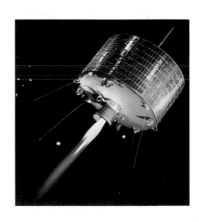

# FLYING TODAY

Running a modern airline is a multi-billion-dollar business. It employs many thousands of people, from planners and engineers to the ground crew who service and maintain planes, and from check in and security staff at the airport, cooks and cleaners behind the scenes, to the crew of the aircraft itself. Provided the demand is sufficient, the faster a plane can be refueled and "turned around", the more money it makes. But many airlines today face severe financial difficulties. In 1992 alone, airlines around the world lost 5.3 billion U.S. dollars.

### Check in
For most flights, passengers must book in advance. They arrive an hour or two before takeoff, to claim their seats, and go through security and passport checks.

### Airline comfort
Today's passenger cabins are easy to service and are roomy enough for passengers to move about in – an important factor since some flights now last more than 20 hours nonstop.

### Airline wars
Like any business, an airline must make money. The battle for passengers is fierce. Pan-American Airlines (Pan-Am) began in 1927, and operated Boeing 707's in the 1950s. But it disappeared in the world recession of the late 1980s and early 1990s. Most countries have a "national" airline. Their advertising appeals to the patriotic feelings of their citizens.

### Bigger and faster
In the 1960s, fast reliable, long-distance aircraft such as the Boeing 707 and the Douglas DC-8 made flying more popular. The Boeing 747 Jumbo Jet, which entered service in the early 1970s, continued the trend. At 320ft long and with a wingspan of 190ft, it is still the world's largest airliner. The double-decker Big Top versions carry over 500 people. Fastest is still the BAC-Aerospatiale Concorde, cruising at 1,350 mph (2,150 km/h), with 130 passengers. Both planes were developed during the 1960s.

Concorde

Boeing 747

## On the ground

A plane must be refueled, serviced (left), and inspected by engineers – all in about 30 minutes. Up-to-date airliners bristle with safety features and safety regulations. The speed and efficiency of emergency services at airports are tested regularly (right).

Cabin staff have been employed on airliners since the 1930s. They serve meals and drinks, and attend to passengers' requests.

## More space

Since the 1960s, plane-makers have tried to fit more people into each airliner, to make it more efficient in terms of fuel and costs. The standard fuselage size, as on the short-distance Douglas DC-9, has been widened on some of the Airbus series, because its jet engines can carry extra weight. The Big Top Boeing 747 has an extended upper cabin behind the flight deck.

Normal fuselage
Douglas DC-9

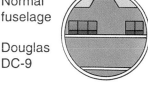

Wide body
Airbus 340

Big Top

Boeing 747-300

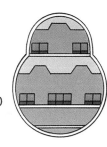

## Security

Planes have become the target for many terrorist threats, both from individuals and from organized terrorist groups. Because of this, security at airports becomes stricter every year. Passengers are questioned about the contents of their luggage, as shown above, and they may be searched. Baggage passes through an X-ray scanner, and suspicious items are investigated.

## An easy target

Terrorism has increased in recent years. The bomb that caused the mid-air explosion of a Pan-Am airliner over Lockerbie, Scotland, in 1988, shocked the world (below). It brought questions about whether planes should transport baggage that does not belong to someone on board. It also raised the issue of whether terrorist warnings, received by airlines almost daily, should all be acted upon, even though most are false alarms.

# THE PLANE-MAKERS

Plane building is big business. The manufacturers Boeing and McDonnell Douglas in the United States and Airbus Industrie in Europe are giant companies. There are arguments as to how much each of these companies is funded either directly or indirectly by its government. At the factory, work proceeds simultaneously on past, present, and future models. Some workers service planes built many years ago, while others research the aircraft of the future.

## Better by design

The invention of computer-aided design (CAD) revolutionized aircraft production. A new plane can have its fuselage widened by an inch or so or be fitted with a new seating layout in a few minutes on screen. Market research on safety and comfort is taken into account, and fuel-economy tests run. Computer programs are not foolproof, and wind-tunnel tests of real scaled-down models show up unforeseen problems.

## Jobs in the industry

In the long term, air travel is continuing to expand, although there have been fat and lean years for the industry. Plane-builders have suffered from world recessions and the fear of terrorism. Computers, automation, and robot workers have meant the loss of many jobs. With the ending of the Cold War, military programs have also faced cutbacks. The EFA Eurofighter currently being developed by teams from Britain, Spain, and Germany was nearly canceled, but was reinstated because about 100,000 jobs were at stake.

The fuselage is made in sections that fit together for riveting and welding.

The fuel pipes, electrical and hydraulic systems in the wings are connected to the flight deck controls.

## Built for strength

Jetliners today have a stressed-skin or single-body construction, pioneered on the Monocoque Deperdussin of 1912. The skin of the central fuselage is built to withstand great pressure, and is strengthened with ribs and hoops to prevent it from bending or collapsing. The fuselage of this European Airbus is joined to the wings, cockpit, and tail sections in the factory in Toulouse, France.

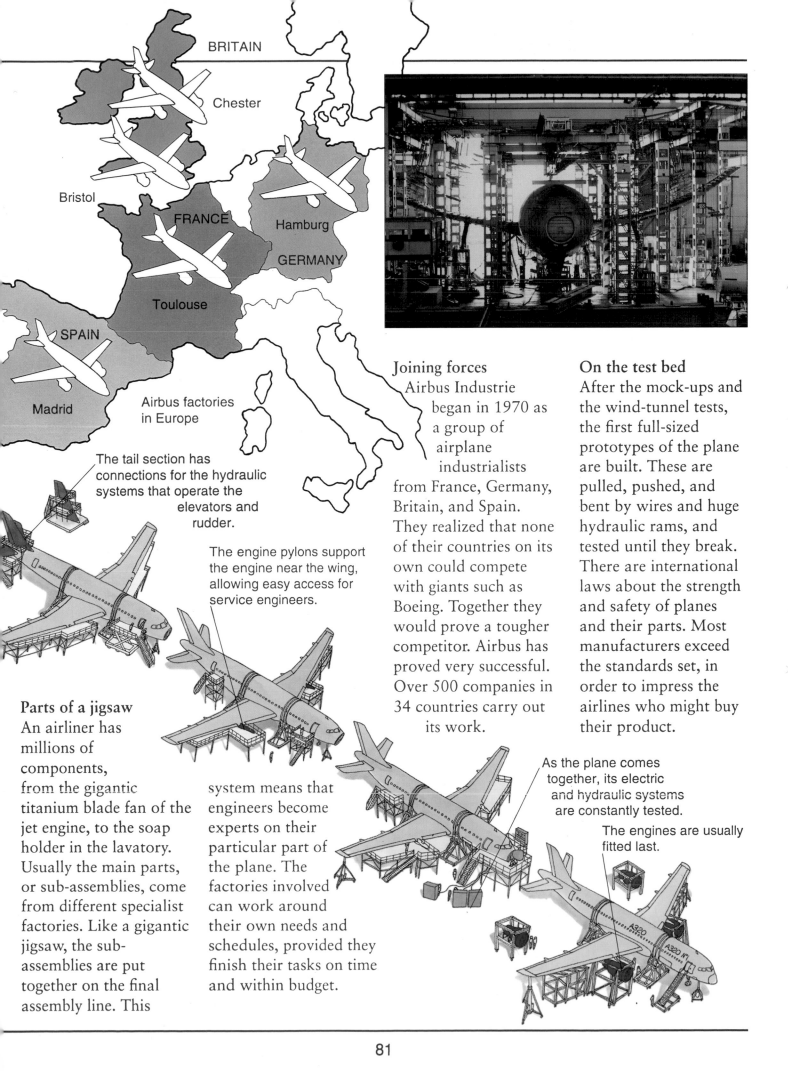

BRITAIN

Chester

Bristol

FRANCE

Hamburg

GERMANY

Toulouse

SPAIN

Madrid

Airbus factories
in Europe

The tail section has connections for the hydraulic systems that operate the elevators and rudder.

The engine pylons support the engine near the wing, allowing easy access for service engineers.

## Parts of a jigsaw

An airliner has millions of components, from the gigantic titanium blade fan of the jet engine, to the soap holder in the lavatory. Usually the main parts, or sub-assemblies, come from different specialist factories. Like a gigantic jigsaw, the sub-assemblies are put together on the final assembly line. This system means that engineers become experts on their particular part of the plane. The factories involved can work around their own needs and schedules, provided they finish their tasks on time and within budget.

## Joining forces

Airbus Industrie began in 1970 as a group of airplane industrialists from France, Germany, Britain, and Spain. They realized that none of their countries on its own could compete with giants such as Boeing. Together they would prove a tougher competitor. Airbus has proved very successful. Over 500 companies in 34 countries carry out its work.

## On the test bed

After the mock-ups and the wind-tunnel tests, the first full-sized prototypes of the plane are built. These are pulled, pushed, and bent by wires and huge hydraulic rams, and tested until they break. There are international laws about the strength and safety of planes and their parts. Most manufacturers exceed the standards set, in order to impress the airlines who might buy their product.

As the plane comes together, its electric and hydraulic systems are constantly tested.

The engines are usually fitted last.

# MILITARY AVIATION

In less than a century warplanes have developed beyond recognition. The first dogfight between two aircraft took place in October 1914. Since then, air power has been decisive in almost every major war. Today's warplanes carry a wide variety of armaments, including fast-firing cannons, and sophisticated guided missiles and bombs. Some planes, such as the Stealth fighter and the F-15 Eagle, are developed for one purpose only. "Multi-role" warplanes are designed to be able to carry out different functions by modifying a basic aircraft frame.

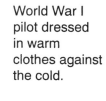

Fokker Dr-1 Triplane, maximum speed 103 mph (165 km/h)

World War I pilot dressed in warm clothes against the cold.

**Early warplanes**
World War I planes were maneuverable but had few technological aids. The pilot relied on his own flying skills. The top flying ace was German pilot Manfred von Richthofen, known as the "Red Baron", (above). His planes – an Albatross, and later a Fokker Triplane – were painted scarlet. Official war records show that he shot down 80 enemy planes, before being killed in 1918.

**World War II**
Different planes had different roles during World War II. Fighters were small and fast, but could not carry many armaments or fly long distances. Bombers such as the Boeing B-29 Superfortress shown here were bigger, with enough fuel for long flights. But they were slower, and vulnerable to enemy fighters.

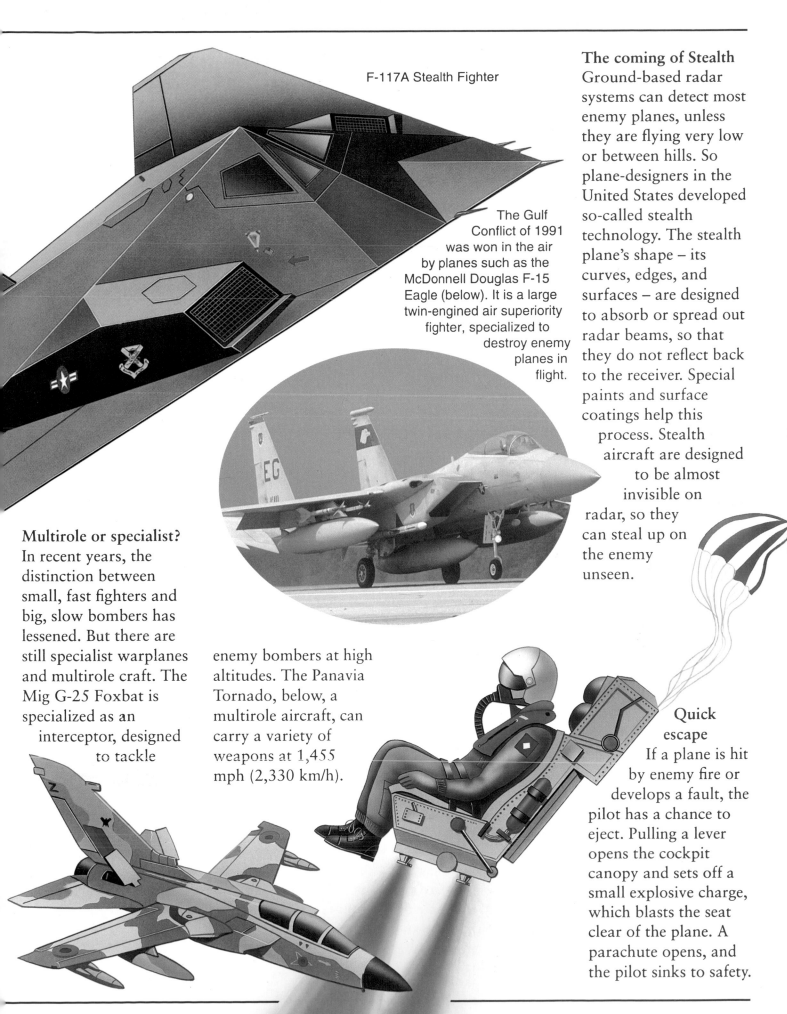

F-117A Stealth Fighter

**The coming of Stealth**
Ground-based radar systems can detect most enemy planes, unless they are flying very low or between hills. So plane-designers in the United States developed so-called stealth technology. The stealth plane's shape – its curves, edges, and surfaces – are designed to absorb or spread out radar beams, so that they do not reflect back to the receiver. Special paints and surface coatings help this process. Stealth aircraft are designed to be almost invisible on radar, so they can steal up on the enemy unseen.

The Gulf Conflict of 1991 was won in the air by planes such as the McDonnell Douglas F-15 Eagle (below). It is a large twin-engined air superiority fighter, specialized to destroy enemy planes in flight.

**Multirole or specialist?**
In recent years, the distinction between small, fast fighters and big, slow bombers has lessened. But there are still specialist warplanes and multirole craft. The Mig G-25 Foxbat is specialized as an interceptor, designed to tackle enemy bombers at high altitudes. The Panavia Tornado, below, a multirole aircraft, can carry a variety of weapons at 1,455 mph (2,330 km/h).

**Quick escape**
If a plane is hit by enemy fire or develops a fault, the pilot has a chance to eject. Pulling a lever opens the cockpit canopy and sets off a small explosive charge, which blasts the seat clear of the plane. A parachute opens, and the pilot sinks to safety.

# VERTICAL TAKEOFF

The modern helicopter took shape in the 1930s. Early attempts at VTOL – Vertical TakeOff and Landing – lifted off the ground, but were unstable. In 1939 Russian-born Igor Sikorsky came up with the experimental VS-300. This pioneering design established the basic layout and control system of the helicopter which has been followed ever since. In the 1950s the invention of the turboshaft engine led to the rapid development of helicopters for many purposes. Today they are used as attack aircraft, transport vehicles, rescue craft, and even for intercity commuting.

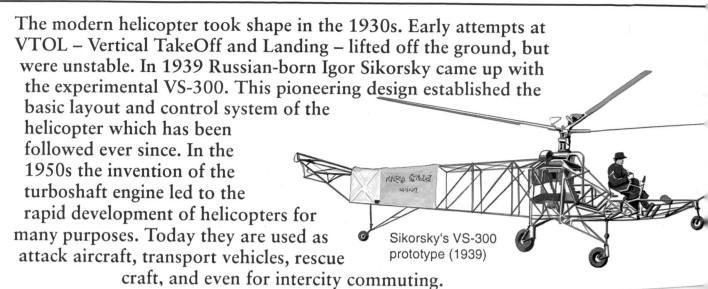

Sikorsky's VS-300 prototype (1939)

**Rotary wings**
The helicopter flies because its wings move fast through the air, rather than the air moving fast over the wings.

Rotor head

Rotor

Main shaft

Gas turbine engine powers rotors.

Pilot's seat

**Lift is provided by rotors** – rotating wings with the typical curved aerofoil shape of a normal plane wing.

Heavy-lift helicopters can transport large loads.

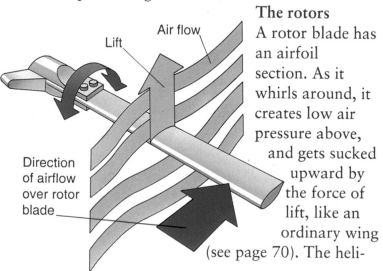

Air flow

Lift

Direction of airflow over rotor blade

**The rotors**
A rotor blade has an airfoil section. As it whirls around, it creates low air pressure above, and gets sucked upward by the force of lift, like an ordinary wing (see page 70). The helicopter's body does not have to move forward for lift to be created. The amount of lift is controlled by the speed of the rotors through the air, and the angle of tilt of their blades, known as the pitch. The pilot adjusts the pitch of the rotors to make the helicopter move forward or backward.

The Boeing Vertol-Chinook

## Best of both worlds?

The Bell-Boeing V-22 Osprey has an unusual design. The engine-and-propeller units at the end of its wings swivel from the horizontal to the vertical. The aircraft uses its rotors to take off vertically like a helicopter, then the units swivel so that the machine flies forward like a normal airplane. This design poses many mechanical difficulties, although prototypes have flown successfully.

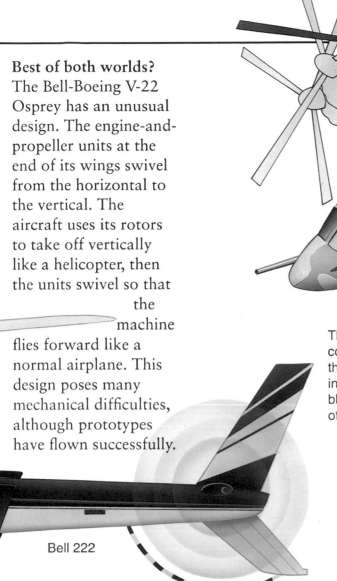

The small tail rotor counteracts the tendency of the helicopter body to rotate in one direction as the main blades spin very fast the other way.

Bell 222

Bell-Boeing V-22 Osprey

## VTOL Jets

The British Harrier "Jump Jet" is an ingenious invention. The thrust of its Pegasus jet engine is directed through four nozzles, two in each side of the fuselage. These can be swivelled to point down for vertical takeoff and hovering, and then backward for normal flight. This makes the Harrier maneuverable and adaptable, and ideal for aircraft carrier use. This very successful design is being built for the US Marines.

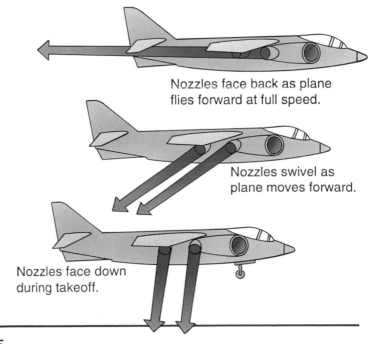

Nozzles face back as plane flies forward at full speed.

Nozzles swivel as plane moves forward.

Nozzles face down during takeoff.

### Search and rescue

The maneuverability of helicopters make them ideal for traffic-spotting, crowd surveys, landing in city centers or other small areas, and SAR (Search And Rescue). They can hover over any type of terrain, from a steep cliff to the open ocean, and winch people by cable to safety.

# SHORT TAKEOFF

Helicopters are versatile flying machines, but are costly to service and maintain. Their fuel consumption is high, especially on longer flights. An alternative is the Short TakeOff and Landing (STOL) plane. STOL craft are designed to use an airstrip of only a few hundred yards. Civilian craft operate from short runways near city centers. Military STOL planes can land on rough airstrips close to front-line troops. On an aircraft carrier, STOL aircraft are launched and landed with the help of a catapult from a runway of just a few dozen yards.

## The autogyro

The autogyro was invented by Spanish engineer Juan de la Cierva in 1923. This tiny flying machine has a small engine that powers a pusher-propeller. The large rotor is not moved by the engine, but turns around by itself. This gives the autogyro a short takeoff run, less than 150 feet in some cases.

## The autorotor

The autogyro's large overhead rotor is pushed around by the flow of air past it, as the craft moves forward. This produces lift, which pulls the autogyro skywards like a helicopter.

## Military STOL

Planes that can fly from short, rough airstrips have long interested the armed forces. Technically, there are two ways to produce an aircraft that can take off in a very short distance. One is to increase the area of the wings, to give more lift. But long, wide wings cause problems at high speed. The other is called lift augmentation, which means increasing the lifting force of a smaller wing in some way. One method is to blow fast-moving air from the engine exhausts over the wing. This gives the effect of the wing moving faster through the air, and so increases lift. Swept-forward wings, as shown in this artist's impression, may help.

## Steep climber

The de Havilland Canada Dash-7 is one of the most successful of the large STOL passenger planes. It has a design typical of STOL aircraft, with wings set high on the fuselage, and a high T-tail. The Dash-7 is powered by four extremely quiet turboprop engines. It carries up to 54 people. The plane can take off in 2,260 feet (690 metres ), becoming airborne so quickly, and climbing so steeply, that many passengers say it is like going up in an elevator!

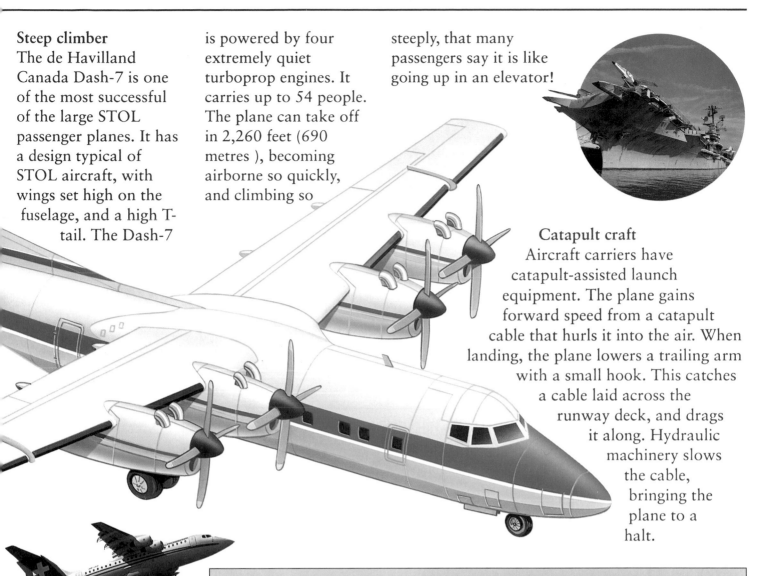

## Catapult craft

Aircraft carriers have catapult-assisted launch equipment. The plane gains forward speed from a catapult cable that hurls it into the air. When landing, the plane lowers a trailing arm with a small hook. This catches a cable laid across the runway deck, and drags it along. Hydraulic machinery slows the cable, bringing the plane to a halt.

The BAe 146, shown above, is a small four-engined jet that combines excellent STOL capabilities with a low level of engine noise.

◀ An artist's impression of a military STOL plane with swept-forward wings is shown opposite.

## Flying into the city

Most large planes need long runways, and create noise that disturbs people nearby. So airports are usually on the city outskirts. It is time-consuming for business travelers to reach these airports. Some cities now have airports almost in the center, such as London's Docklands Airport. STOL aircraft use the short runway, and climb rapidly so their noise soon fades.

# WORK AND PLAY

The past 20 years have seen an enormous growth in private flying. There are now many ways to fly for fun, but all amateur pilots must pass examinations before they are let loose in the skies. Generally the cheapest aircraft are the smallest. Tiniest of all powered craft are microlights, which are like motorized hang-gliders and can pack onto a car. Working planes perform many different tasks, in addition to carrying passengers and freight.

Ailerons

## Hang-gliders
The modern hang-glider has a lightweight frame of metal tubes and cables, and a flexible wing of air-proof, tear-proof material. The pilot controls the glider by shifting his or her body weight.

Lightweight construction

## One-person planes
Amateur fliers do not necessarily need to spend large amounts of money on their sport, since many craft are owned by clubs, and can be hired by the hour or day. Piloting a plane by yourself, alone in the sky, can be an exhilarating experience. Training takes place in a two-seater version, where the instructor demonstrates the basic controls and how to navigate.

## Gliders
A glider has long, thin wings for sustained, soaring flights. It has no engine, so must be winched into the air on a long cable or towed up by a powered craft. A glider always sinks in relation to the air around it. But it can gain height in relation to the ground by spiraling in rising currents of air known as thermals.

Clear cockpit cover

## Gaining height
Air moves upward as it blows against a slope. Or it may rise where it is warmed by bare rock. The pilot circles in this updraft, and so gains height.

## Kit planes

It is possible to build a plane in a space the size of a living room! Plane kits are less expensive than ready-made planes, because money is saved on assembly. The purchaser builds and assembles the plane, which can be enjoyable in itself. But such craft must be thoroughly checked and certified before they can be flown.

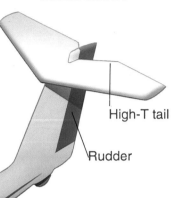

High-T tail

Rudder

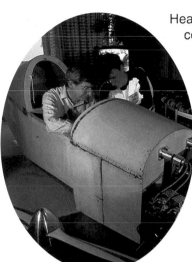

Heat-proof collar around envelope

Burner

The wickerwork gondola absorbs the shock of landing

## Baldooning

The balloon consists of a passenger basket and an envelope of tough fabric, which is filled with hot air. Warm air is lighter than cool air, and so rises, lifting the balloon. The heat comes from a flame roaring from a burner, fueled by propane gas in metal bottles.

## Bizjets

Traveling by scheduled flights takes time. Some companies have their own executive planes. These small aircraft carry about 10-14 passengers at cruising speeds of 500 mph (800 km/p). Travelers may use the telephone, fax, and computer on board.

## Working planes

The Canadair CL-215 is an adaptable transport plane, available in many versions. One is specialized for fire-fighting (shown right). It can skim over a lake or sea and scoop up over 1,100 gallons (5,000 liters) of water, then dump this onto a fire. Small planes fitted with spraying or dusting bars can quickly spread pesticides (below).

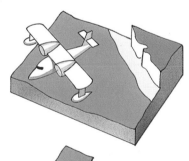

# INTO THE FUTURE

What is the future of flight? Vast amounts of money and resources are used in the design and construction of each new plane. Military users have pioneered many advances in aircraft technology, but with the ending of the Cold War, military projects face cutbacks. Flying is a fast way to travel, but is inefficient in terms of fuel consumption compared to road, rail, or ship. Aircraft pollute the high atmosphere with their exhaust gases, and the skies around airports with their noise and smell. But millions of people are employed in the air industry, and millions more rely on the privilege of air travel for business and vacations.

## Bigger planes?

Some flight experts predict that planes will get even bigger. It is more economical to carry lots of passengers in one huge plane than in several small planes. This works well for long-haul (long distance) routes. There is also a future for smaller, quieter, and economical commuter aircraft that hop between city centers. Passenger planes are becoming ever more specialized for different jobs.

Artist's impression of Boeing 747 super double-decker

## Too big

The Hughes H4 Hercules flying boat was designed and built by American billionaire Howard Hughes. Its wingspan was 320 feet (97.5 meters). Called the "Spruce Goose" because of its sprucewood construction, it flew only once, in 1947, with Hughes at the controls. It was simply too large, and its engines too weak.

## Busier skies?

People who live near major airports suffer noise, smell, and extra traffic. Airlines want easier travel for their customers, but local residents want a peaceful, less polluted life. These requirements bring the two sides into conflict. These protesters in Japan are campaigning against a new airport, which they feel could blight their lives.

## Bigger airports?

As more people travel by air, so airports have to cope with them. If planes accommodate more passengers in the future, there may be even longer queues at ticket checks, passport controls, and baggage reclaim. Airport designers face problems similar to those in huge sports stadiums, where thousands of people come and go in a rush, then the building is left almost empty. And there are always the considerations of safety and security.

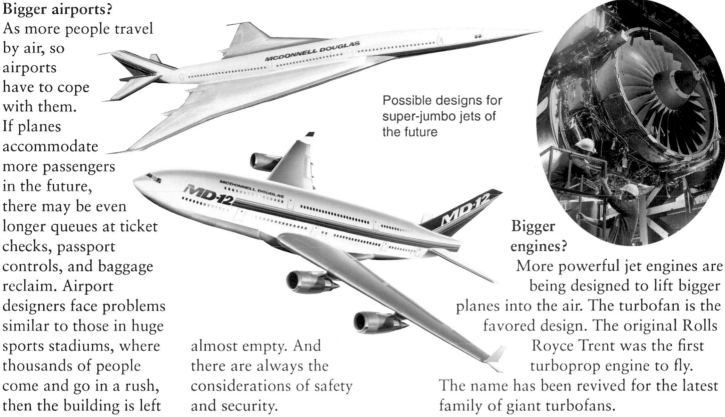

Possible designs for super-jumbo jets of the future

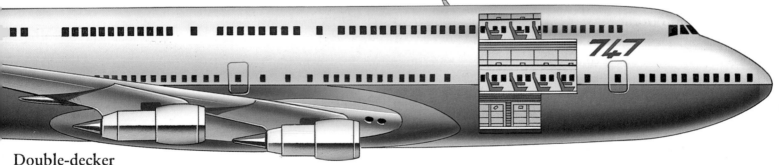

## Bigger engines?

More powerful jet engines are being designed to lift bigger planes into the air. The turbofan is the favored design. The original Rolls Royce Trent was the first turboprop engine to fly. The name has been revived for the latest family of giant turbofans.

## Double-decker

A proposal for the Boeing 747 Jumbo Jet is to make the whole fuselage double-decked, to accommodate over 800 passengers. But more powerful engines would be needed to carry the extra weight.

## Space-planes

Plane-makers are exploring the possibility of craft that could fly in space, but take off and land using a normal runway. One proposal, the British HOTOL (HOrizontal TakeOff and Landing), has special engines that work conventionally in Earth's atmosphere and as rockets in space. The project may prove too costly, with not enough demand. Surveys show that most people are content to fly at normal speed and altitude, and take a few hours extra, rather than see billions of dollars spent on a project with limited benefits to the very few.

Artist's impression of HOTOL

# The Book of GREAT INVENTIONS

# INTO
# SPACE

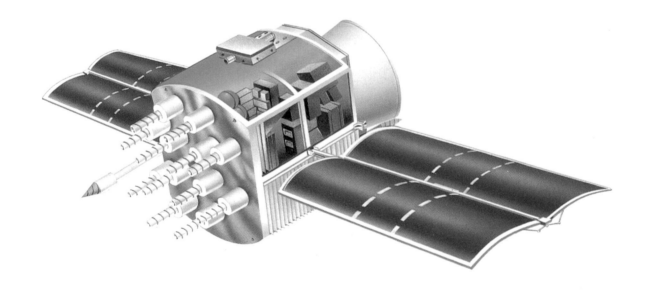

# CONTENTS

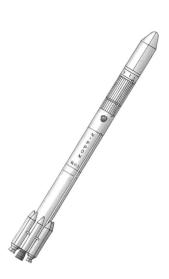

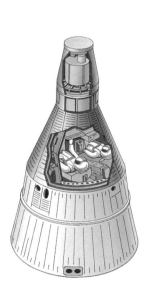

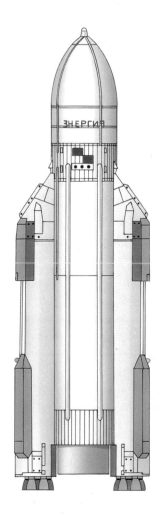

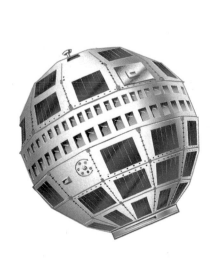

# SPACE TODAY

Since the Space Age began in 1957, space has become a huge industry driven by pride, prestige and hope of profit. Men have stood on the Moon, while satellites and space probes have explored distant planets. On Earth, space science has changed daily life. Communications satellites bring TV pictures and inexpensive telephone calls from around the world. Manufacturers use technology and materials developed for spacecraft. But would all this have happened without the Cold War, and will it continue now harmony has broken out? This chapter looks at what space exploration has achieved and the impact it has had and will have on our daily lives.

**The final frontier**
Space enthusiasts say that space travel is our last great challenge. It may one day reveal incredible knowledge. Opponents say it wastes billions of dollars that could be used to relieve hardship in the world and uses vital resources.

**Space junk**
After thirty years of launches, dead satellites, jettisoned hatches, old booster rockets, and miscellaneous junk now orbit the Earth in a thickening cloud. In the popular orbits used by communications satellites, space now has to be rationed out by international agreement.

Buran

Maneuvering rockets

**Dangers**
Space flight may endanger the lives of ordinary people. Satellites have crashed to Earth in large pieces. Their radioactive cargoes can spill over the land. Some, like this anti-missile satellite (left) may carry laser weapons.

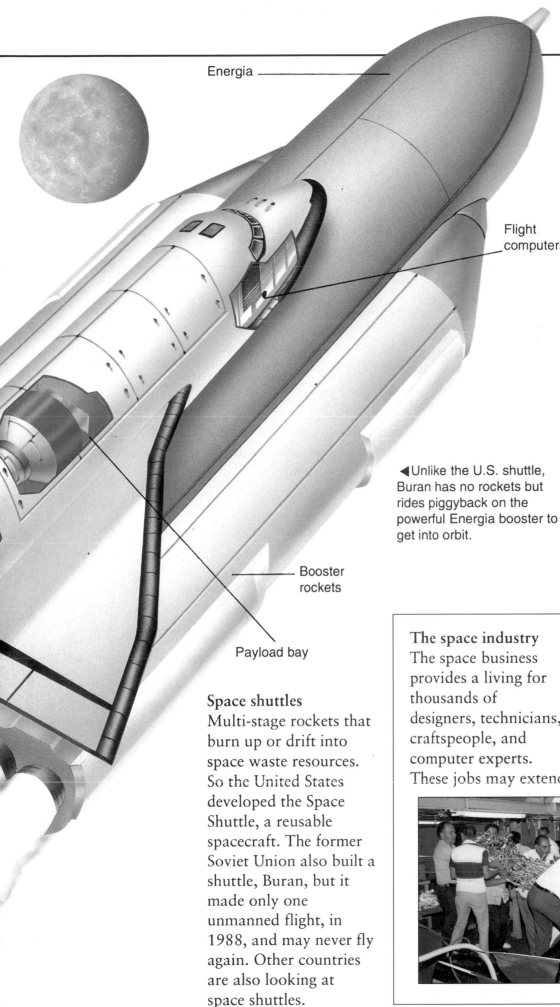

Energia

Flight
computers

◀ Unlike the U.S. shuttle,
Buran has no rockets but
rides piggyback on the
powerful Energia booster to
get into orbit.

Booster
rockets

Payload bay

### Space shuttles
Multi-stage rockets that burn up or drift into space waste resources. So the United States developed the Space Shuttle, a reusable spacecraft. The former Soviet Union also built a shuttle, Buran, but it made only one unmanned flight, in 1988, and may never fly again. Other countries are also looking at space shuttles.

### Medical advances
Monitoring the health of astronauts in space helps doctors understand how the human body works. In space, you grow one to two inches taller and your wrinkles disappear, thanks to weightlessness. With no exercise, your muscles and bones weaken. These changes are not permanent.

### The space industry
The space business provides a living for thousands of designers, technicians, craftspeople, and computer experts. These jobs may extend into space itself. Without gravity, it may be possible to make better products than on Earth. Crystals grow better, and some drugs are easier to manufacture.

# DREAMS OF SPACE TRAVEL

The first rockets were made in China in the 13th century. From the beginning, rockets were used as weapons of war, to carry explosives and target an enemy. By 1806, rockets were being used against Napoleon's fleet, but they were inaccurate. In the early 20th century two men dreamed of using rockets to travel into space: Konstantin Tsiolkovsky, a Russian, and Robert Goddard, an American. Independently they realized that only the rocket, which carried all its own fuel with it, could escape the pull of Earth's gravity, and travel across the vast emptiness of space.

### Tsiolkovsky's idea
Konstantin Tsiolkovsky, a schoolteacher, worked out the basic principles of space flight around 1903. He realized that to escape the Earth's gravity, several powerful rockets would be needed. These rockets could be arranged in stages, each stage taking over as the other ran out of fuel.

### Goddard
Robert Goddard, an American physicist, was the first to design a proper high-altitude rocket. After people laughed at his early efforts, he worked more secretly at his launch pad in Roswell, New Mexico.

### German interest
In the early 1930s, the German Army became interested in developing rocket-powered missiles. An early result of their experiments was the VFR rocket (below).

Goddard's first rocket was launched on March 16, 1926 (right) at Auburn, Massachussetts. It burned gasoline and liquid oxygen, to create hot gases that blasted downward and thrust the rocket upward. The rocket is the tiny object at the top. It rose just 40 feet in the air and flew 184 feet in two and a half seconds, before falling back to Earth once again.

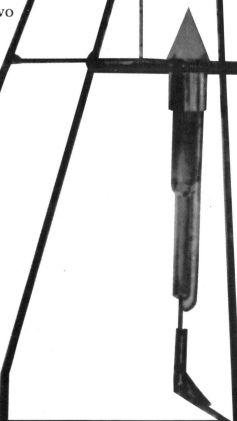

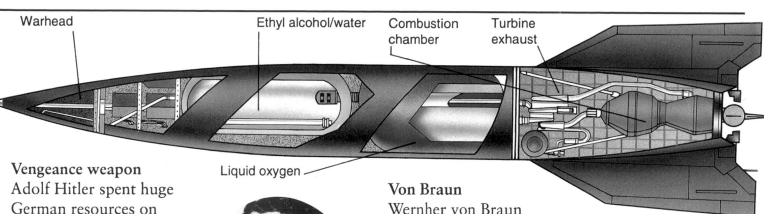

Warhead

Ethyl alcohol/water

Combustion chamber

Turbine exhaust

Liquid oxygen

## Vengeance weapon

Adolf Hitler spent huge German resources on rockets. In 1942 the prototype A-4 rocket reached a height of 95 miles from the launch pad at Peenemunde on the Baltic Sea. An A-4 later became the first man-made object to leave the Earth's atmosphere. It was also known as the V-2, the V for Vergeltingswaffe, or vengeance weapon.

## Von Braun

Wernher von Braun (left) became leader of the German rocket team designing missiles. During World War II, 1,403 V-2s were fired at London, killing 2,754 people. After the war von Braun went to the United States, became an American citizen, and helped build the first American rockets.

## The V-2 in action

The V-2 used a steam turbine to pump alcohol and liquid oxygen from separate tanks into the rocket motor. Here the gases mixed and fired in a continuous explosion that blasted the rocket forward. But the V-2 was not very accurate.

## Space fiction

The inspiration for Von Braun and many others came from writers like Jules Verne. Verne wrote a story about a voyage to the Moon as early as 1865, anticipating many of the features of the Apollo Moon landings 100 years later. H.G. Wells, in *War of the Worlds* portrayed an invasion of Earth by intelligent but unfriendly creatures from Mars.

# THE SPACE AGE BEGINS

World War II ended in 1945, but the "Cold War", an era of confrontation between the United States and the Soviet Union, began soon after. Both countries developed rockets to display their military might and national pride. Under a brilliant leader, Sergei Korolyev, the Soviets had by 1956 built a giant rocket, the SS-6, capable of carrying a two-ton bomb 4,000 miles. To demonstrate the rocket, Korolyev was ordered to launch a satellite, a small object that would stay in space, circling round the Earth. On 4 October 1957, the satellite Sputnik 1 was launched. The Space Age had begun.

## Launchers

Sputnik's SS-6 launcher was big and simple, but very effective. It consisted of a central core, with four strap-on boosters to increase lift-off power.

Compared to the soviet design, the American rockets (below) were lighter and more delicate in construction. They used high-technology fuel tanks rather than the thick-walled steel tanks of the SS-6. Less power meant that American satellites had to be light. This gave a boost to the development of miniaturized electronic devices such as new transistors, which were soon used in portable radios and other everyday objects.

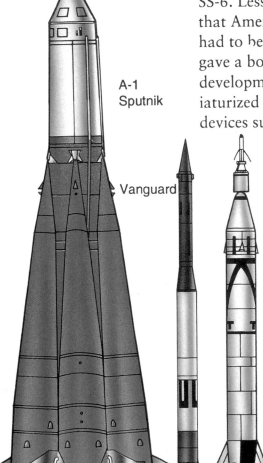

A-1
Sputnik

Vanguard

Juno 1

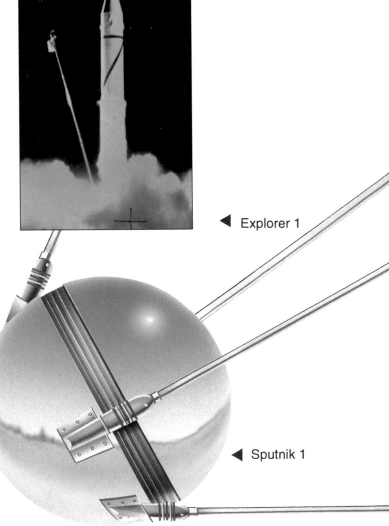

◄ Explorer 1

◄ Sputnik 1

## The response to Sputnik

By late 1957, the United States was ready to match Sputnik with a satellite of its own. But the first launch, of a Vanguard rocket with a tiny 3.4 pound satellite, was a dismal failure. It rose only a few feet before crashing back to the launch pad and exploding in a ball of flame. In desperation, the United States turned to Wernher von Braun, whose satellite project had been in need of money.

## American success

Von Braun put together a Jupiter C rocket and a satellite called Explorer. This was launched successfully on January 31, 1958 (see the photo on the opposite page). Explorer 1 was a much smaller satellite than either of the first two Sputniks which preceded it into space. Other early American launches met with less success: a Mercury rocket suffered premature engine cut-off during its launch in 1960 (above left).

In April 1958, the National Aeronautics and Space Administration (NASA) was created, to survey the Moon and put a man into space. It has been a force in world science and politics ever since.

▲ NASA's first office building in Washington D.C.

## Sputnik

Sputnik 1 (left) was a simple metal sphere that weighed 184 pounds. Its transmitter emitted a series of beeps. In November 1957, the much larger Sputnik 2 carried a passenger: the dog Laika, who became the first space traveler.

## The van Allen belts

One of the instruments on Explorer 1 was designed to count and measure electrically charged particles in space. This instrument led to the first space discovery. James van Allen, the scientist responsible, noticed that at certain heights the counter seemed to stop working, and he realized it had been overloaded. The reason was a region in space dense with charged particles – now known as the van Allen belts. These sometimes disrupt radio communications.

## Voices from the sky

A satellite is an object that goes around another. Scientists realized that artificial radio satellites could relay radio, TV, and telephone signals around the Earth. The first was Telstar, (below right) launched by the U.S. in 1962. In 1965, Early Bird became the first geostationary satellite. People could watch the Beatles(below) live on TV beamed from another continent.

# THREE, TWO, ONE, LIFT-OFF!

Early in 1959, the Soviet Union began building a spacecraft to carry a man into orbit. Vostok ("East") was designed to be virtually automatic in operation, so that unmanned launches to test its systems could be carried out first. After two successful test launches, Yuri Gagarin was shot into space on April 12, 1961, made a single orbit of the Earth and ejected at a height of 23,000 feet before parachuting down. A human being had entered space for the first time, an event as historic as the voyage of Christopher Columbus.

**Mercury and Gemini**
In 1961, the United States succeeded in putting men in space. John Glenn achieved a complete orbital flight the next year. These early flights were in one-person Mercury space-craft. After the United States declared its intention of making a manned Moon landing, two-man Gemini spacecraft were used to develop skills, like docking, needed for the lunar mission.

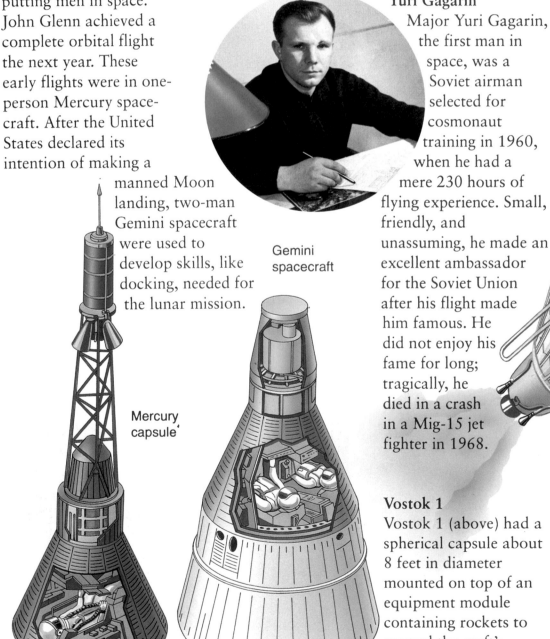

Mercury capsule

Gemini spacecraft

**Yuri Gagarin**
Major Yuri Gagarin, the first man in space, was a Soviet airman selected for cosmonaut training in 1960, when he had a mere 230 hours of flying experience. Small, friendly, and unassuming, he made an excellent ambassador for the Soviet Union after his flight made him famous. He did not enjoy his fame for long; tragically, he died in a crash in a Mig-15 jet fighter in 1968.

**Vostok 1**
Vostok 1 (above) had a spherical capsule about 8 feet in diameter mounted on top of an equipment module containing rockets to control the craft's position and to slow it down for reentry. At the time the Soviet Union declared that Gagarin had stayed in his capsule until landing, to give the impression that their space program was more advanced.

**Cost of manned flight**
Each manned launch costs hundreds of millions of dollars. Astronauts' vehicles are large, heavy, and fitted with life support systems. They need still more powerful launchers and more preparation.

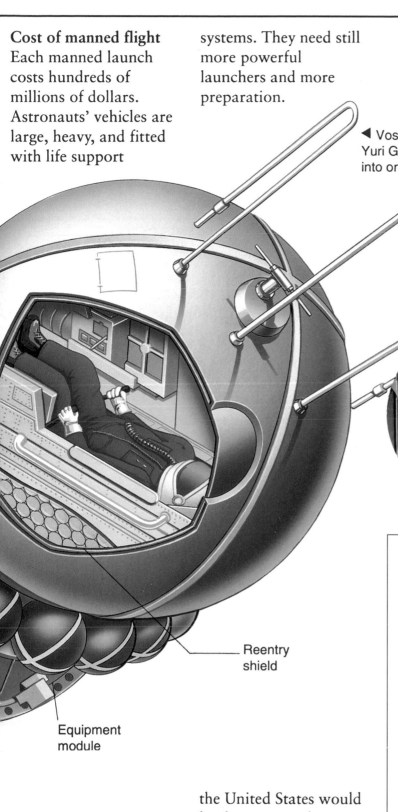

Reentry shield

Equipment module

◀ Vostock 1 carried Yuri Gagarin into orbit

▶ The Vostok capsule preserved in the Moscow space museum

▼ Painting of the launch of Vostock 1

**Soviet success**
In 1964, the USSR put three men into orbit in Voshkod 1. On Voshkod 2 in 1965, Alexsei Leonov made the first space walk, then struggled to get back into the spacecraft. After landing 1,800 miles off course, the crew spent a night hiding from wolves before rescue.

**The space race**
The Soviet manned missions were a huge propaganda success. The American people became concerned that they were being left behind by the only nation powerful enough to threaten them with war. The government voted money for space programs, and 5,000 people jammed Central Station to watch John Glenn become the first U.S. astronaut.

**Kennedy's promise**
President John F. Kennedy, looking for a popular crusade to mark his presidency, asked for the Moon. On May 25, 1961 he promised that the United States would land a man on the Moon, and return him safely to Earth, before the decade was out. These were bold words, for America had not yet succeeded in putting a man into orbit.

# MAN ON THE MOON

NASA's Apollo Moon-landing program was a triumph of organization and technology. It required a new rocket, a new spacecraft, and a new plan for landing on the Moon and then departing safely. The rocket was the three-stage Saturn V, designed by Wernher von Braun. The spacecraft was Apollo, which could divide into two while in Moon orbit, leaving the command module aloft while two explorers descended to the surface in the lunar module. In July 1969, it all worked flawlessly. Kennedy's promise was kept, and men set foot on the Moon for the first time.

## Rehearsals

A series of missions tested every aspect of the Apollo design. The first flights, Apollo 5 and 6, were unmanned; Apollo 7 took men into Earth orbit, Apollo 8 into lunar orbit. Apollos 9 (right) and 10 tested the lunar module, first around the Earth and then in lunar orbit. Finally all was set for the first landing by Apollo 11. There were five more Moon landings.

## Setbacks

Though mainly successful, the Apollo program had its failures. In 1967, a fire in Apollo 1 (above) on the launch pad killed three astronauts. In 1970 an explosion on Apollo 13, two days after launch meant the Moon landing was canceled, and the astronauts only just managed to return safely to Earth.

## Lunar takeoff

One key to the success of the Apollo mission was a reliable rocket to lift the lunar module from the surface of the Moon. Without it, the astronauts would have been trapped. When the first design proved troublesome, a new one was created.

**▼ Rocket power**
The Saturn V rockets when launched created the loudest sound man has ever produced – 190 decibels. Their five first-stage engines burned 15 tons of fuel a second.

Five J-2 engines

Five F-1 engines

First stage

## Landing conditions

The nature of the Moon's surface was something which concerned American scientists. Some thought it consisted of a layer of dust 30 feet thick that would swallow Apollo. Unmanned flights by Surveyor spacecraft proved this was not the case, and sent back pictures of the surface.

## Lunar experiments

On the Moon, Armstrong and Aldrin set up a laser reflector to enable scientists to measure the distance to the Moon to within 6 inches. They also set up instruments to study "moonquakes," and collected rocks to bring back to Earth.

Launch escape system

Command module

Service module

Lunar module

Third stage

J-2 engine

Second stage

## Studying the Moon

The astronauts traveled in an electrically-powered Lunar Rover to examine the landscape. Six Apollo landings found that the Moon was a dead planet 4.6 billion years old, with a deeply cratered surface and rolling hills.

## One giant leap

"One small step for man, one giant leap for mankind", said Neil Armstrong as he set foot on the Moon on July 21, 1969. Millions watched on live TV back on Earth. Alongside him was Buzz Aldrin, while Michael Collins waited in the orbiting command module.

## Neil Armstrong

Neil Armstrong was a test pilot who had served in the Korean War. A cool, careful flyer, his skill helped Apollo land safely when he changed course at the last minute to avoid rough ground.

## Link-up

In 1975, NASA agreed to a joint space mission with the Soviet Union, in which an Apollo and a Soyuz spacecraft would link in orbit. This "handshake in space" was to begin a new era of cooperation. The mission went well, and U.S. and Soviet astronauts shared a meal (below).

# LAUNCH VEHICLES

Throw a ball in the air and it will come down, pulled by the force of gravity. Throw it hard enough and it will never come down, because it has enough speed to escape Earth's gravity and fly into space. This is the job of a rocket-powered launch vehicle. In theory, one giant rocket could reach space, but it would be carrying unnecessary weight as it reached the edge of space. In a multi-stage rocket, each stage falls away as it runs out of fuel, leaving a lighter rocket to fly higher.

### Into orbit

Three rocket stages are enough to reach space (below). Strap-on boosters may be used as part of the first stage. They provide extra power during the first part of the flight, when gravity is strongest. When they burn out they are jettisoned and fall into the sea. The second and then the third stages of the rocket burn to bring the cargo or payload – in this case, satellites – to orbiting height.

### Early rockets

The first American manned launches were made by Redstone rockets, a development of the V-2. For the orbital flights the more powerful Atlas rocket was used.

### Launch vehicles

Only the United States and the Soviet Union have developed rockets powerful enough for manned missions. The biggest is the Soviet Energia (below right and inset opposite) which can lift 100 tons into Earth orbit. Other nations have built smaller rockets for launching satellites, including Ariane 4 (center) produced for the European Space Agency (ESA). Japan has a satellite launcher (left) and is planning a manned space program.

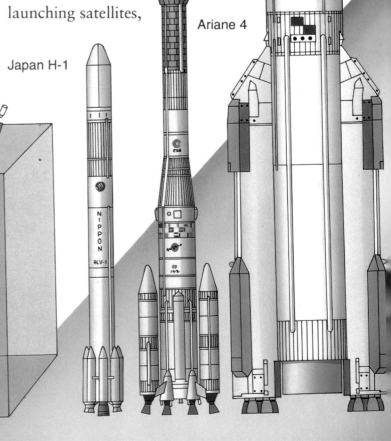

Energia

Ariane 4

Japan H-1

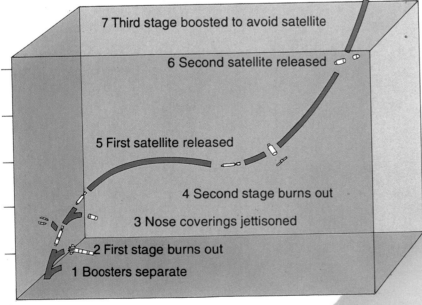

7 Third stage boosted to avoid satellite

6 Second satellite released

5 First satellite released

4 Second stage burns out

3 Nose coverings jettisoned

2 First stage burns out

1 Boosters separate

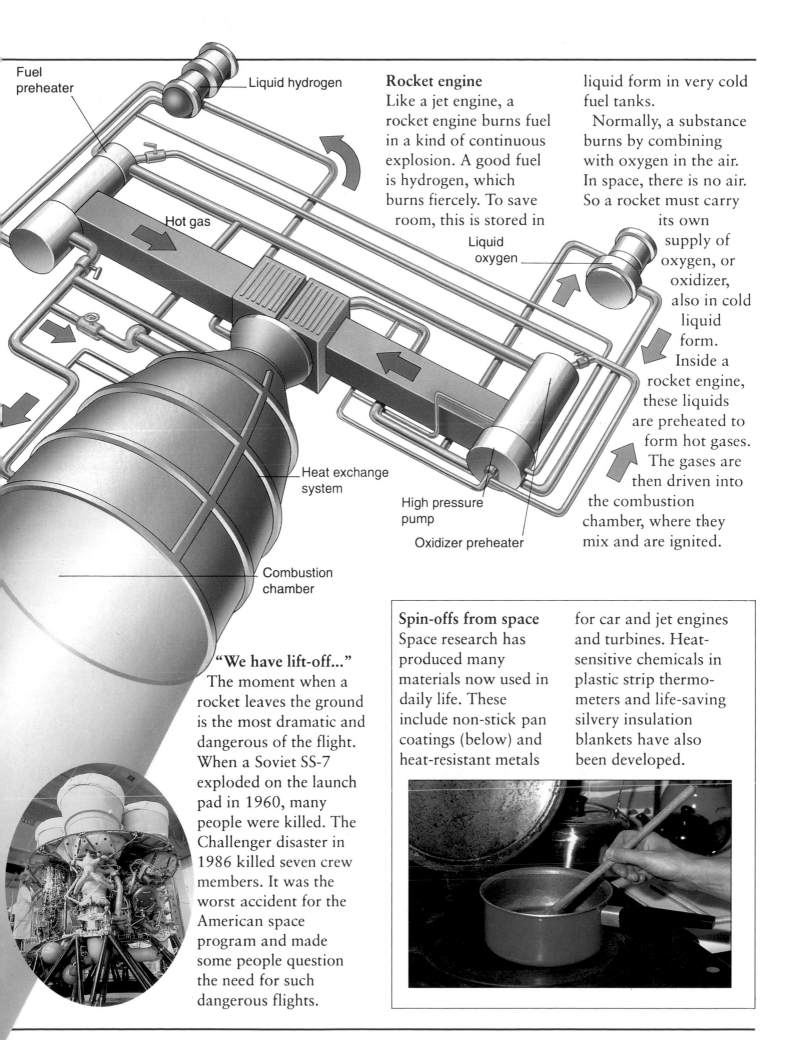

Fuel preheater

Liquid hydrogen

Hot gas

Liquid oxygen

Heat exchange system

High pressure pump

Oxidizer preheater

Combustion chamber

## Rocket engine

Like a jet engine, a rocket engine burns fuel in a kind of continuous explosion. A good fuel is hydrogen, which burns fiercely. To save room, this is stored in liquid form in very cold fuel tanks.

Normally, a substance burns by combining with oxygen in the air. In space, there is no air. So a rocket must carry its own supply of oxygen, or oxidizer, also in cold liquid form. Inside a rocket engine, these liquids are preheated to form hot gases. The gases are then driven into the combustion chamber, where they mix and are ignited.

## "We have lift-off..."

The moment when a rocket leaves the ground is the most dramatic and dangerous of the flight. When a Soviet SS-7 exploded on the launch pad in 1960, many people were killed. The Challenger disaster in 1986 killed seven crew members. It was the worst accident for the American space program and made some people question the need for such dangerous flights.

## Spin-offs from space

Space research has produced many materials now used in daily life. These include non-stick pan coatings (below) and heat-resistant metals for car and jet engines and turbines. Heat-sensitive chemicals in plastic strip thermo-meters and life-saving silvery insulation blankets have also been developed.

# THE REUSABLE SPACECRAFT

Conventional rockets are used just once, then thrown away. The space shuttle is different; it takes off vertically, like a rocket, enters space as a spacecraft, and then returns and lands on a runway like an aircraft. The idea was to make spaceflight simpler and cheaper, but the results have been disappointing. To put a satellite into orbit with NASA's space shuttle costs up to $250 million, no less than a conventional rocket. The popular dream of ordinary people paying for a space ride is still many years away.

## Development

The design of the shuttle drew on experience from a series of rocket planes developed in the United States. The first of these, the Bell X-1, launched in mid-air from beneath a B29 bomber, was the first aircraft to exceed the speed of sound in 1947. Later models (below) showed the rounded shape and V-shaped delta wings of the shuttle, designed to resist the intense heat of reentry and then to glide swiftly to a landing.

### X-15

The Bell X-15 rocket plane (above), tested in the 1960s, reached speeds of more than 4,000 mph and attained heights of 67 miles, the very edge of space.

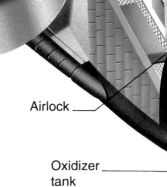

Satellite payload

Fuel tanks

Payload handling controls

Airlock

Oxidizer tank

X 24A

M2F3

X 24B

## The shuttle

The shuttle is built of aluninum alloy, covered with ceramic tiles to protect it from the heat of reentry. The cargo bay is 60 feet long by 15 feet wide, which is about the size of a railway freight wagon. The doors are made of carbon-fiber reinforced plastic. The stubby wings allow the shuttle to glide, though very fast, and land at more than 200 mph The flight deck is the upper level at the front, with the galley and sleeping berths below in the mid deck area. Each shuttle costs about $1.1 billion.

## First flight

The space shuttle Columbia lifted off for its maiden flight in 1981. In general, the shuttle program has been successful. It launches satellites regularly, carries out experiments, and also does secret military work. It also repairs satellites in orbit.

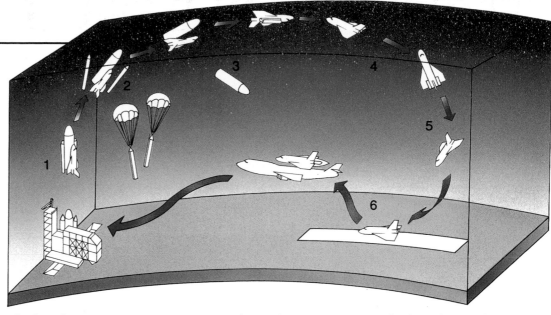

## Flight plan

The sequence of the shuttle appears above. For lift-off (1), the shuttle uses its three main engines, plus two boosters. Fuel is carried in a huge internal tank. After two minutes, the boosters burn out and parachute into the sea (2). Six minutes later, the main engines stop, and the fuel tank is released (3). The final step into space is made by smaller orbital engines (4). After landing (5), a Boeing 747 returns the shuttle to the launch pad (6).

## International rescue

In 1992 (below) three shuttle astronauts spent more than eight hours on a space walk, wrestling a four-ton communications satellite, Intelsat-VI, into the cargo bay. There they fitted a new rocket motor and sent the satellite off on its true orbit, 22,300 miles above the Earth.

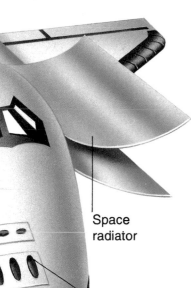

Space radiator

Forward control thrusters

Nose wheels

## Disaster

In America's worst space disaster, hot gases leaked through a joint in the booster casing during the launch of Challenger in 1986. A tongue of flame burned into the main tank and ignited the fuel, blowing the shuttle to pieces and killing its seven crew members, among them Christa McAuliffe, a teacher. The disaster set back the program by nearly three years, as engineers struggled to prevent it from ever happening again.

# ROCKETS FOR RENT

Today, space has become big business. Rockets can be rented from several suppliers, to launch commercial satellites into orbit. The main players are NASA and the European Space Agency, but Japan, China and what remains of the Soviet space organization are also interested in the market. After a poor start, ESA's Ariane launchers have proved very reliable. The Challenger disaster of 1986 slowed the United States' effort, and opened up the market. By early next century, ESA hopes that Ariane 5 will be able to put a manned European shuttle, Hermes, into space.

## Equator launch

The Ariane launch site is at Kourou in French Guyana (right). A rocket launched close to the Equator takes greatest advantage of the Earth's speed of rotation, so needs less thrust than it would if launched from Europe. Surrounded by jungle, the Kourou site has three launch pads, assembly buildings and a control center (below).

## Different payloads

A rocket's cargo is its payload. Commercial rockets carry a huge variety of payloads, including satellites for scientific research, communications, navigation, monitoring the weather, and mapping the Earth. Sometimes more than one satellite can be launched on the same mission, sharing costs (right).

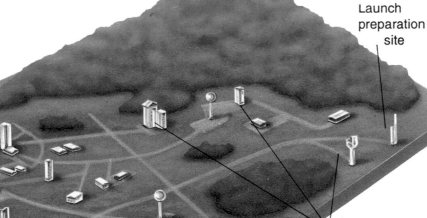

Launch preparation site

Booster integration building

Launch pads

Control center

Final assembly building

## Military launches

Some 2,000 military satellites have been launched by the United States alone in the past 20 years. Many military launches are kept secret, but usually involve satellites for spying, military communications, or precise navigation. Spy satellites have tended to increase confidence between the superpowers.

## Italian space program

In 1988, the Italian government set up the Italian Space Agency, with a budget of more than $1 billion for its first two years. The agency is responsible for Italy's own satellites and for taking part in ESA programs. One of Italy's satellite and communications centers is sited near Palermo, Sicily (above). Its Marcos satellites are designed to study the atmosphere.

ESA
Giotto
satellite

### Historic Launches

| Launch | Type | Date |
|---|---|---|
| Sputnik (USSR) | demonstration | 10/4/57 |
| Explorer 1 (US) | scientific | 1/31/58 |
| Ariel-1 (UK) | scientific | 4/26/62 |
| Telstar 1 (US] | 1st commercial comsat | 7/10/62 |
| Early Bird (Intelsat) | comsat | 4/6/65 |
| Osumi (Japan) | 1st Japanese satellite | 2/11/70 |
| Landsat 1 (US) | Earth resources | 7/23/72 |
| Meteosat (Europe) | weather satellite | 11/23/77 |
| Seasat 1 (US) | sea resources satellite | 6/27/78 |
| Intelsat 5 | telecomms satellite | 12/6/80 |
| Arabsat | telecomms satellite | 2/8/85 |
| SPOT 1 (France) | remote sensing | 2/22/86 |

## International interest

Britain, France, Canada, Germany, India, Brazil, and Japan (inset below) all have special interest in satellites.

Japan's
H-1
rocket

Proposed
Hermes
space
orbiter

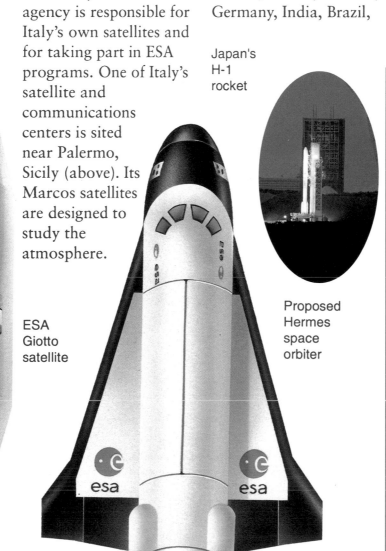

## Microchip technology

The demand for electronic devices on board satellites has been a great stimulus to the development of microchips, now found in a huge range of consumer products, from pocket TVs to laptop computers. These devices have increased the capacity and reliability of weather, communications, military, and spy satellites.

# LIVING IN SPACE

While the United States planned Moon missions and shuttles, the former Soviet Union was concentrating on manned space stations and space probes to the planets. Soviet cosmonauts hold all the records for endurance in space. Colonel Yuri Romanenko, the most experienced space traveler of all, has spent more than a year of his life in space, on three separate missions. The most recent was aboard the Mir space station, launched in February 1986. Since its launch Mir has been continually occupied by a series of crews sent up in Soyuz spacecraft, the first permanent manned outpost in space. The cosmonauts spend their time carrying out experiments and making observations of the Earth.

## Skylab

The Skylab space station (below and right), made from an empty Saturn IVB rocket tank, was put into orbit in 1973. It was an unlucky craft, requiring a tricky space walk to unfold its solar panels. It finally reentered the atmosphere, breaking up over Australia. It was in orbit for six years but in use for only six months.

## Close companions

Living for months in a small space can be difficult. Yuri Grechko and Romanenko (on the left in the circular photo opposite) agreed to share responsibility for routine tasks and mistakes.

## A 24-hour day

Although there is no day or night, astronauts keep to a 24-hour routine, which suits the human body best.

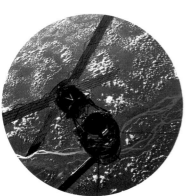

## A change of staff

Soyuz transfer craft for changing crews dock on one of the docking ports on the end of the Mir station. A fuel tanker is docked at the other end.

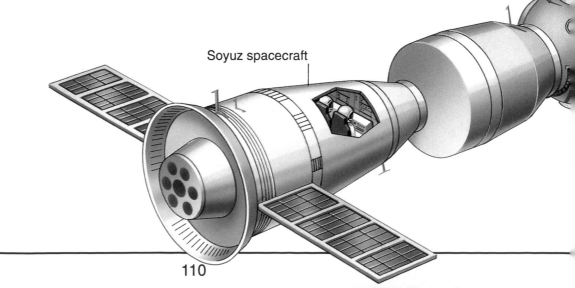

Soyuz spacecraft

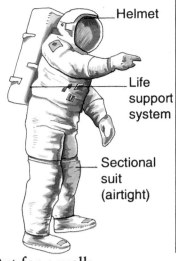

Helmet

Life support system

Sectional suit (airtight)

### Keeping fit in space
The bones of early space dwellers became brittle, and their muscles wasted away. They had problems readjusting to gravity on Earth. Today, astronauts counteract these effects through exercise and regular medical checks (right).

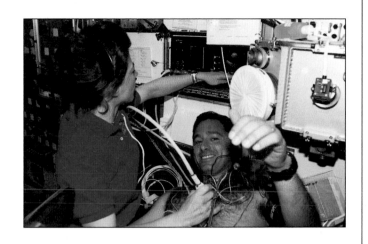

### Out for a walk
For space walks astronauts wear a pressurized space suit, usually with a back-pack (above). It contains supplies of oxygen, as in the case of the Apollo lunar explorers, or small gas jets for moving about, in the Manned Maneuvering Unit (MMU).

### Space sickness
Living in space affects some astronauts quite badly, causing sickness for the first few days. This is due to the brain receiving strange messages from the balance organs inside the ears.

Airlock

Working and dining table

Meteorite shield

Unmanned tanker

### ◄ Space station Mir
Mir is about 36 feet long and 14 feet in diameter. Most of it is living accommodation for a crew of two. Its large solar panels convert sunlight to electricity.

# SATELLITE REVOLUTION

Today, 35 years since Sputnik went into space, there are hundreds of satellites in orbit around the Earth. They relay telephone conversations and TV pictures, take pictures of clouds and weather systems, observe the fine detail of the Earth, and provide precise navigational information for ships and planes. Live TV pictures bounce around the world in a miracle of communication that we now take for granted. The satellite revolution is the single most important result of the conquest of space.

Antenna reflector

## Deployment

The space shuttle launches satellites from many countries (the one shown below is Mexico's Morelos satellite). They are lifted from its cargo bay with a jointed manipulator arm 50 feet long. Once the satellite has been released and the shuttle has moved a safe distance away, a small rocket on the satellite is fired to move it into position for orbit. This final stage is called deployment.

Antenna feed

Fixed forward solar panel

Thermal radiator

Control thruster

Propellant tank

Traveling wave tube amplifier

Battery pack

Extendible rear solar panel

## Predicting the weather

To provide weather forecasts, satellites take pictures of clouds and even hurricanes (right). They measure temperature, humidity, and wind speeds.

## Satellite control

Once in orbit, a satellite's exact position can be adjusted by small control thrusters. These are fired by remote control, using radio signals from ground engineers, if the satellite drifts out of position. The solar panels, dishes, and other antennae are folded up to save room during the launch. They are unfolded through radio signals sent from the ground station.

## How satellites work

The curvature of the Earth makes long-distance communication difficult, since the waves carrying radio or TV signals travel in straight lines. Satellites act like radio masts thousands of miles high. They pick up signals from ground stations and beam them back down. A modern communications satellite, or comsat, can handle dozens of TV channels or thousands of telephone calls at once. On the ground, signals from satellites are received by satellite dishes (below).

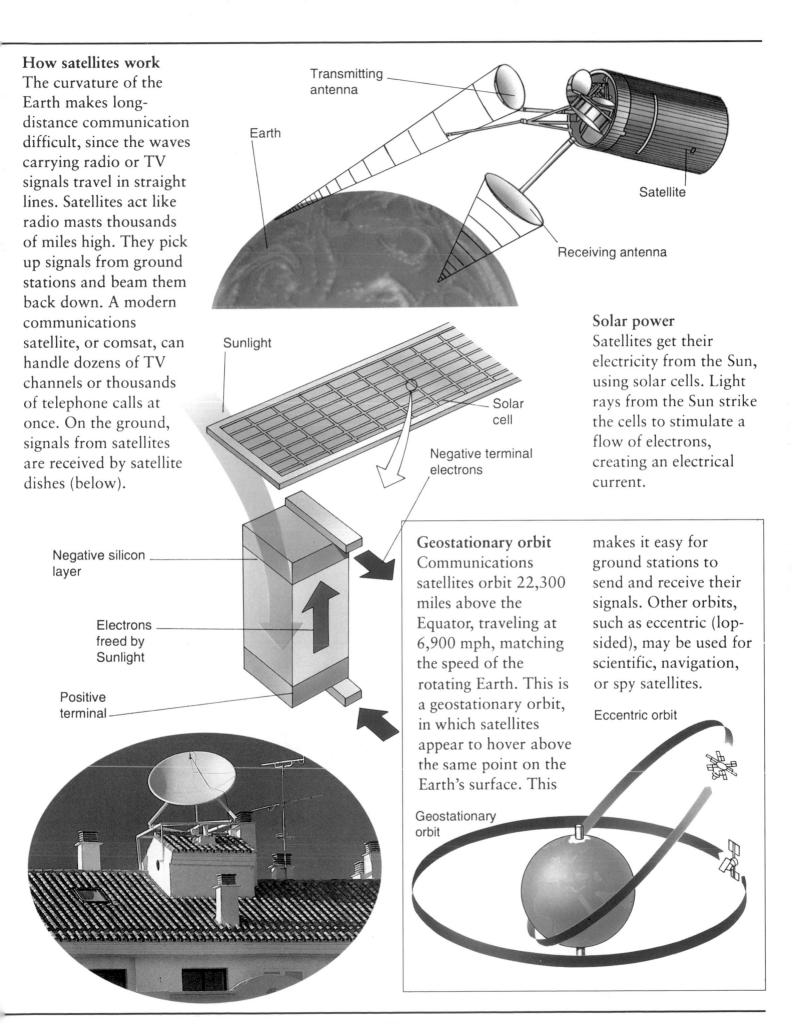

Transmitting antenna

Earth

Satellite

Receiving antenna

Sunlight

Solar cell

Negative terminal electrons

## Solar power

Satellites get their electricity from the Sun, using solar cells. Light rays from the Sun strike the cells to stimulate a flow of electrons, creating an electrical current.

Negative silicon layer

Electrons freed by Sunlight

Positive terminal

## Geostationary orbit

Communications satellites orbit 22,300 miles above the Equator, traveling at 6,900 mph, matching the speed of the rotating Earth. This is a geostationary orbit, in which satellites appear to hover above the same point on the Earth's surface. This makes it easy for ground stations to send and receive their signals. Other orbits, such as eccentric (lopsided), may be used for scientific, navigation, or spy satellites.

Eccentric orbit

Geostationary orbit

# SPIES IN THE SKY

Good generals always try to seize the high ground, and there is nothing higher than a satellite. At least a third of all space launches are military in purpose. Without spy satellites, the intelligence services of the major powers would know very little. Nuclear submarines could not operate without navigation satellites. Secret military communications also depend on satellites. The outcome of recent wars, from the Falklands to the Gulf, has been greatly affected by the use of satellites.

## Seeing from space

The clarity of the view from space is remarkable, as is evident from this satellite picture of the fire at the Chernobyl nuclear reactor in 1986. Spy satellites probably cannot read car number plates on Earth, as is often claimed, but they can certainly pick out individual vehicles and even people. Their orbits are often arranged so that they pass over the same spot on the ground when the Sun is in the same position each day, so that changing light and shade do not confuse the images.

## Under cover

When the space shuttle carries military payloads (below), a veil of secrecy is drawn over the mission. The U.S. military even built its own shuttle launch pad at Vandenberg Air Force Base in California, to launch the shuttle on spy missions. It will never be used; the Challenger disaster and other shuttle delays made the military chiefs decide to use ordinary rockets.

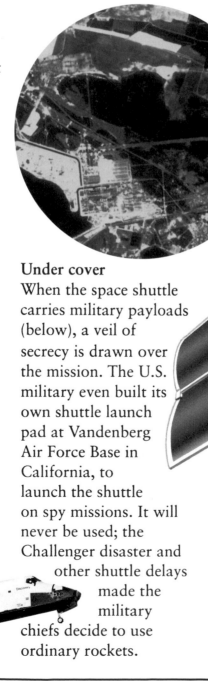

Rocket motor

Solar panel

Control thruster

## Navstar

If nuclear submarines' missiles are to hit their targets, they must know where they are firing from with absolute precision. The U.S. Navstar system was launched in the 1980s. It stands for NAVigation System using Time and Ranging. Each satellite contains three atomic clocks. The system works by measuring the time taken for the signal broadcast by the satellite clocks to reach the user on the ground.

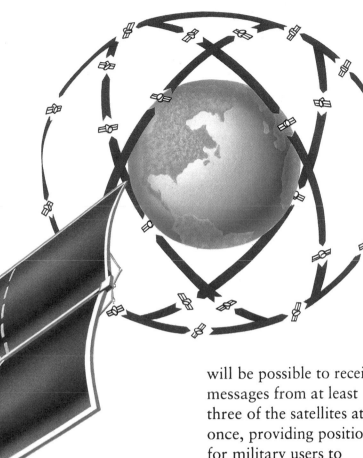

## The Gulf War

During the Gulf conflict in 1991, American spy satellites provided vital intelligence about the position and movements of the Iraqi troops occupying Kuwait. Two types of satellite were used: low-orbit ones with telescopes and cameras to take detailed pictures of troop concentrations, airfields (below) and missile launcher sites, and geostationary ones to pick up Iraqi radio, radar, and other signals. Iraq had no such satellites, so was at an enormous disadvantage.

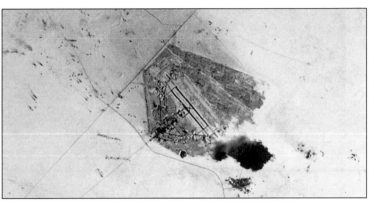

## Navstar orbits

Navstar will ultimately have about 20 satellites in three orbits 12,500 miles up. From any point on the Earth, it will be possible to receive messages from at least three of the satellites at once, providing positions for military users to within 30 feet. Civilians can also use Navstar, but not at the same precision; they will know their position to within 300 feet.

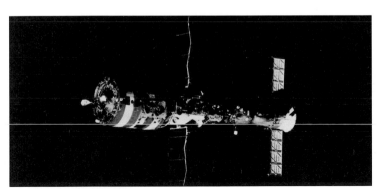

## Military Salyuts

The Soviet Union launched at least three Salyut space stations devoted to military work. They contained a camera instead of the telescope in the normal Salyut, and the cosmonauts provided information for military exercises as they happened live. Hundreds of unmanned Soviet spy satellites have also been flown.

## SDI

The United States' Strategic Defence Initiative, or "Star Wars," was to be a space-based system for destroying enemy missiles in flight. Announced in 1983, SDI envisaged the use of high-power guns, ground-based rockets, and laser and particle beam weapons. It was an ambitious plan. SDI tests achieved some successes, including shooting down an unmanned aircraft with a laser. The collapse of the USSR in the 1990s has meant that SDI has been scaled down.

# SECRETS OF THE UNIVERSE

At a fraction of the cost of manned spaceflight, the planetary probes have uncovered far more information in the past 30 years than had been learned in the previous 300. Pioneer 5 was America's first deep space probe, launched in 1960. Mariner 2 was the first probe to visit another planet, Venus, in 1962. Vikings 1 and 2 landed on Mars in 1976. Voyagers 1 and 2 visited the outer planets, taking over ten years to get there. NASA's Hubble space telescope is looking further out into the universe than any Earth-based instrument can.

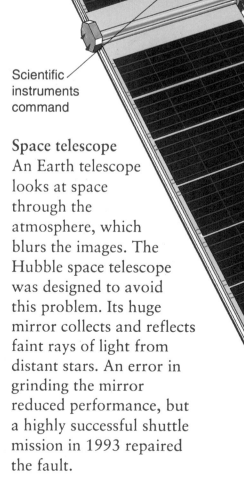

Antenna

Solar panels

Light shield

Scientific instruments command

## Peering into space

Space experts and enthusiasts alike have always been intrigued by the possibility of life elsewhere in the universe. NASA is to use radio telescopes in the biggest-ever search for intelligent extraterrestrial life. They will listen to radio signals from stars like our own Sun in the hope of picking up a radio "beacon" from other beacons.

▼ The radio telescope at Arecibo, Puerto Rico, has the largest dish in the world.

## Origins of the universe

Space research has led some physicists to believe that they are close to understanding how the universe began, with the "Big Bang" theory. Professor Hawking of Cambridge University (below) has researched "black holes," areas of space from which nothing – not even light – can escape.

## Space telescope

An Earth telescope looks at space through the atmosphere, which blurs the images. The Hubble space telescope was designed to avoid this problem. Its huge mirror collects and reflects faint rays of light from distant stars. An error in grinding the mirror reduced performance, but a highly successful shuttle mission in 1993 repaired the fault.

## The Voyager program

The two Voyagers launched in 1977 have explored the huge outer planets, Jupiter, Saturn, and Uranus. More than 15 years after launch, the satellites are still working well, though their signals are growing dim as they slip out of the solar system into interstellar space.

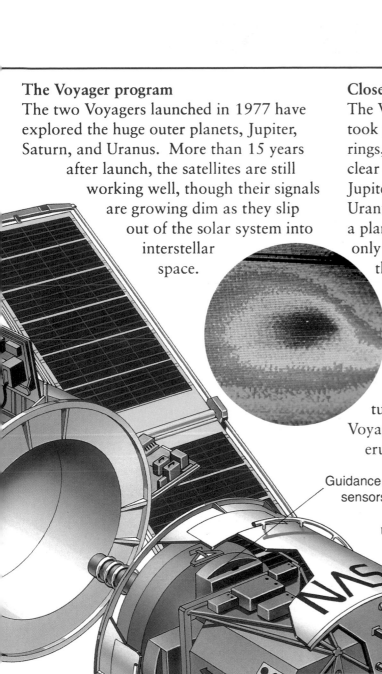

## Close-ups of the planets

The Voyager spacecraft took pictures of Saturn's rings, and made the first clear observations of Jupiter (right) and Uranus. Around Jupiter, a planet made of gas only slightly denser than water, Voyager 1 identified 16 moons. These ranged from the icy wastelands of Callisto and Ganymede to the turbulence of Io, where Voyager 1 observed a volcano erupting.

Voyager 2 confirmed that Uranus has rings and found ten previously unknown moons. It traveled on to Neptune, where it found another six moons and took a picture of the Moon Triton, one of the coldest objects in the solar system. Halley's comet (inset left above) was observed by the Soviet probe Vega 1, in 1986.

Guidance sensors

Equipment section

Optical telescope

▼ NASA's Hubble can look into deep space.

## Studying the Sun

Satellites have helped our understanding of the Sun, without which life on Earth would not exist. Scientists have studied the solar wind – the flow of charged particles from the Sun. Pictures of solar flares taken by Skylab (left) show the turmoil that exists on the solar surface.

# THE FUTURE OF SPACE

What next for the space industry? The United States is considering two major projects. One is a permanently manned space station in Earth orbit. The other is a manned trip to Mars. Neither will be easy or cheap. In general, space exploration is very expensive. The Apollo project cost $25 billion; by 1980, the Soviets had spent $45 billion on space missions. With the end of superpower rivalry, space budgets are likely to be cut, since there is less need for rocket missiles or intensive satellite spying. The practical advantages of a permanently manned space station to our everyday lives are doubtful. Manned space flight faces an uncertain future, though unmanned satellites will continue to flourish.

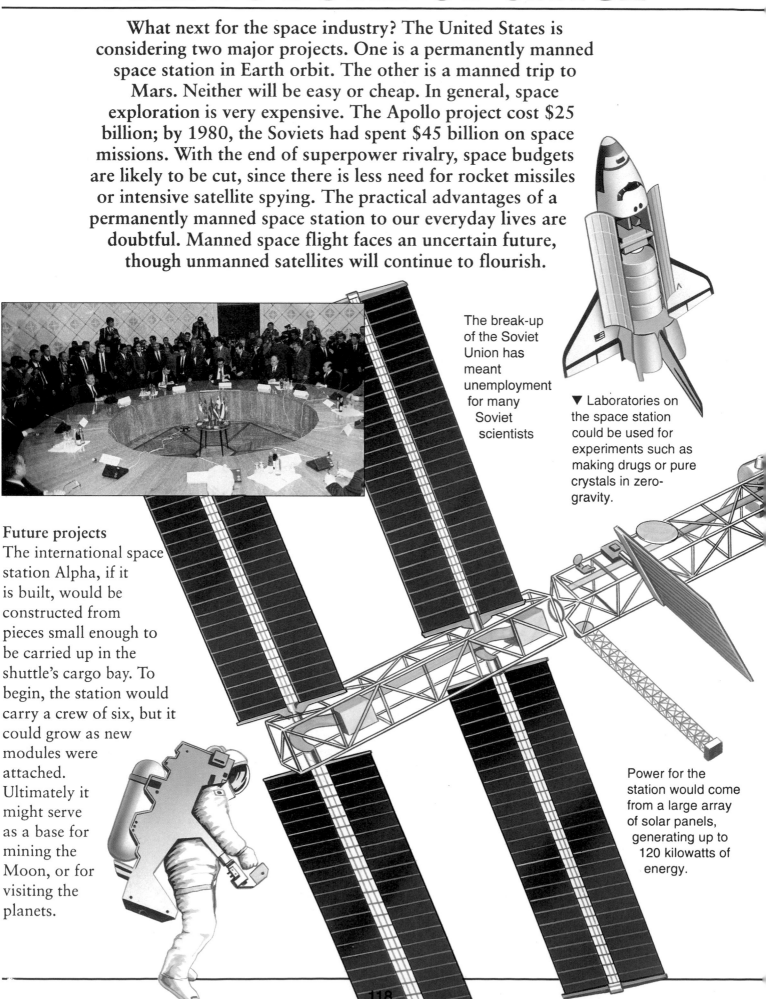

The break-up of the Soviet Union has meant unemployment for many Soviet scientists

▼ Laboratories on the space station could be used for experiments such as making drugs or pure crystals in zero-gravity.

**Future projects**
The international space station Alpha, if it is built, would be constructed from pieces small enough to be carried up in the shuttle's cargo bay. To begin, the station would carry a crew of six, but it could grow as new modules were attached. Ultimately it might serve as a base for mining the Moon, or for visiting the planets.

Power for the station would come from a large array of solar panels, generating up to 120 kilowatts of energy.

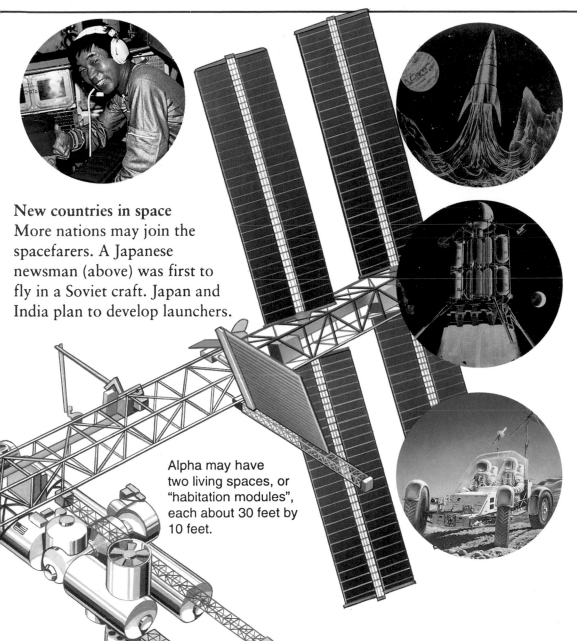

### New countries in space
More nations may join the spacefarers. A Japanese newsman (above) was first to fly in a Soviet craft. Japan and India plan to develop launchers.

Alpha may have two living spaces, or "habitation modules", each about 30 feet by 10 feet.

### Predictions
Many predictions about space travel have come true: multi-stage rockets and men walking on the Moon, although not quite as conceived in these illustrations from 1927 (top) and 1953 (center). Other predictions have proved false, like the claim by the American astronomer Percival Lowell that there is life on Mars. Today, predictions still flourish. One is that life will be found elsewhere, but it may be billions of miles away. Another is that we may make Mars habitable by changing its climate and creating a breathable atmosphere. More realistically, spaceplanes may carry passengers halfway around the Earth in a few hours, and astronauts may explore and mine the Moon (left).

### Employment
Huge numbers of people have been employed in the space and defense industries, which now face a diminished future. In the former Soviet Union, thousands of space scientists are unemployed. In the West the situation is not so acute, but the days of dramatic, prestige-creating space spectaculars may be over.

### Fuels of the future
To reach any planet in a reasonable time, a rocket would need a new form of propulsion. The best prospect is the nuclear rocket, in which heat from a reactor creates a jet of gas to propel the spacecraft. Traveling outside the solar system (right) remains a dream.

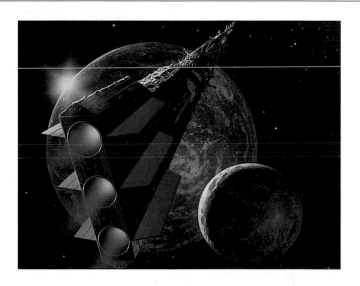

# CHRONOLOGY OF SHIPS AND BOATS

▲ Thor Heyerdahl's *Ra II*

**c.40,000 B.C.** Aborigines may have reached Australia aboard sea going boats.

**c.7,000 B.C.** Reed boats begin to be used on the rivers of Mesopotamia and Egypt.

**c.3,000 B.C.** Simple square sails begin to be used on the Nile river in Egypt.

**c.500 B.C.** The trireme, an oar-powered warship, is developed in the Mediterranean.

**c.285 B.C.** The earliest known lighthouse is built at Alexandria in Egypt.

**c.100 B.C.** The Chinese begin using the sternpost rudder on their junks.

**c.200 A.D.** Arab boat-builders begin using multiple masts and lateen sails, which allows sailing with the wind from the side.

**c.800** The Vikings begin using their longboats to make raids and voyages around the North Sea.

**c.1100** The Chinese are already using magnetic compasses to navigate.

**c.1300** The Chinese begin building ships with watertight bulkheads.

**1400-1500** The fully rigged ship, with three masts and a mixture of square and lateen sails, is developed in Europe.

**1492** Christopher Columbus lands in the West Indies.

**1498** Vasco da Gama reaches India by ship, opening up trade routes to the East from Europe.

**1620** The first submarine is launched.

**1758** Captain John Cambell invented the sextant, allowing sailors to calculate latitude.

**1820's** The first clippers, the pinnacle of sailing design, are launched in America.

**1836** The screw propeller, an alternative to the paddle wheel, is

▲ A cross channel hovercraft

patented by Francis Pettit Smith.

**1838** Isambard Kingdom Brunel's *Great Western* makes its first trip across the Atlantic.

**1860** H.M.S. *Warrior*, the first all iron battleship, is launched.

**1869** The Suez Canal, is opened to shipping.

**1897** Sir Charles Parsons demonstrates *Turbinia*, the world's first stream turbine-powered vessel.

**1900** The first hydrofoil is built.

**1906** H.M.S. *Dreadnought*, forerunner of the modern warship, is launched.

**1912** The White Star Line's *Titanic* sinks on her maiden voyage, with the loss of more than 1,500 people.

**1914** The Panama Canal is opened.

**1915** Sonar is developed to detect submarines.

**1918** H.M.S. *Argus*, the first purpose-built aircraft carrier, is launched.

**1934** The liner, Queen Mary, is launched from Scotland.

**1955** Christopher Cockerell invents the hovercraft.

**1970** Thor Heyerdahl sails from Africa to the West Indies in *Ra II*, a boat made from papyrus reeds.

**1985** The deep submergence vessel, *Sea Cliff*, reaches a depth of 20,000 feet.

**1989** The oil tanker, *Exxon Valdez*, runs aground in Alaska.

**1993** The final Global positioning System (GPS) satellite goes into space.

▲ The *Queen Mary*

# CHRONOLOGY OF THE CAR

**1885** Karl Benz makes his three-wheeled engine-driven carriage, the first practical car.
**1886** Gottlieb Daimler builds a four-wheeled car with a gasoline engine.
**1891** Daimler's Mercedes model becomes the first true "car" as we would recognize it today.
**1893** First U.S. gasoline-powered automobile

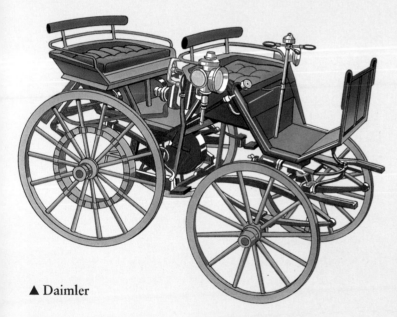

▲ Daimler

built by the Duryea brothers.
**1895** André and Edouard, the Michelin brothers devise pneumatic tires.
**1904** Automatic transmission fitted by Sturtevant in the U.S.; Michelin bring in tire tread patterns for better grip in the wet.
**1906** Charles Rolls and Henry Royce introduce the Silver Ghost.
**1908** Henry Ford makes

the first Model Ts.
**1910** A public drive-in "gas station" opens in Detroit, Michigan.
**1912** First cars fitted with electric starters, making cars "more popular with the ladies."
**1913** Ford introduces the moving assembly line.
**1913** The first direction indicators (swinging arms).

**1915** The first windshield wipers offered on Cadillacs.
**1919** Three color traffic lights are introduced in Detroit.
**1921** Hydraulic (pressure-oil) systems fitted to the Duesenberg Model A.
**1923** Pratts (later Esso) put lead additives in gasoline.
**1929** The first synchromesh gearbox is fitted to a production

car, by Cadillac.
**1934** The new Citroën has a monocoque chassis construction, independent suspension and front-wheel drive.
**1935** Parking meters appear in Oklahoma City.
**1937** Windshield washers are fitted to some Studebakers.
**1938** Germany launches the KDF, or Volkswagen "Beetle."
**1944** U.S. establishes its interstate highway system.
**1949** The first large tail-fins appear on Cadillacs.
**1950** Dunlop patents a new type of disk brake.
**1951** Power steering becomes standard on many quality cars.
**1957** Fuel injection is fitted to ordinary production cars.
**1959** BMC launch the revolutionary Mini.
**1961** The Renault R4's cooling system is sealed for life.
**1966** Electronic fuel systems developed.

▲ Austin Tourer

**1968** U.S. introduced first laws to control car exhaust pollutants.
**1969** Experiments are made with and air bag that inflates to protect the driver in a crash.
**1971** Engines are modified to use unleaded gasoline.
**1974** New cars in America have catalytic converters.
**1977** Experiments with hydrogen gas as a fuel.
**1984** Mercedes-Benz brings in ABS (Anti-Lock Braking System).
**1987** Sunraycer solar-powered car crosses Australia using rechargeable silver-zinc batteries.
**1990** Electric cars are launched by Peugeot and Fiat.

▲ Ford Thunderbird (T-Bird)

# Chronology of Flying Machines

**1783** First manned ascents, in Montgolfier hot-air balloons.
**1849** George Cayley experiments with gliders.
**1874** Frenchman Félix du Temple's steam-powered craft almost becomes airborne.
**1891-96** Otto Lilienthal

solo from England to Australia.
**1932** Amelia Earhart is first woman to fly the Atlantic solo nonstop.
**1935** First flight of the Douglas DC-3 Dakota.
**1937** *Hindenberg* crash ends the airship era.
**1937** Test-bench firings of Frank Whittle's Unit

▲ Apache helicopter

▲ Charles Lindberg's plane, *Spirit of St. Louis*

makes many successful gliding flights.
**1900** First Zeppelin airship flies in Germany.
**1903** First flight in a true airplane by Wright brothers.
**1909** First plane flight across the Channel, by Louis Blériot.
**1910** First regular air service by airship, between Germany and Sweden.
**1919** First nonstop plane flight across the Atlantic, by Alcock and Brown.
**1927** First solo trans-Atlantic flight by Charles Lindberg.
**1930** Amy Johnson is the first woman to fly

No. 1, first jet engine.
**1939** Igor Sikorsky designs and flies the VS-300 helicopter.
**1939** First flight by a jet plane, the Heinkel He178, in Germany.
**1940** Boeing Stratoliner is first airliner with pressurized cabin.
**1945** U.S. Airforce B-29 Superfortresses drop atomic bombs on Japan ending World War II.
**1947** Charles Yeager is first to fly supersonic in Bell X-1 rocket plane.
**1949** Maiden flight of first passenger jetliner, de Havilland Comet.
**1954** Maiden flight of Boeing 707 jetliner.
**1967** Bell X-15 rocket

plane becomes the fastest winged craft at 4,520 mph (7,274 km/h)
**1969** Maiden flights of first supersonic jetliner, Concorde, and Boeing 747 Jumbo.
**1972** First flight of Airbus A300 prototype.
**1976** Lockheed sr-71 A Blackbird sets speed record for a jet plane, at 2,193 mph (3,529 km/h).
**1986** Dick Rutan and Janet Yeager are first to fly round the world nonstop in *Voyager*.
**1987** Airbus A320 uses "fly by wire."
**1988** Terrorist bomb destroys PanAm Boeing 747 flight over

Lockerbie, Scotland.
**1989** First flight of Northrop B-2 Stealth Bomber.
**1992 October** Israeli Boeing 747 crashes killing 70.
**December** Dutch DC-10 crashes, killing 54.
**December** Libyan Boeing 727 crashes, killing 158.
**1993** Boeing 747 Cargo engine locking pins are redesigned after crashes.
**1995 June** New satellite navigation system enables flight distances to be cut.
**June** Lockheed Martin and Boeing unveil the pilotless spy-plane, *Darkstar*.

▲ Airbus A300

# CHRONOLOGY OF SPACE

**1903** Konstantin Tsiolkovsky publishes his scientific paper on the use of rockets for space travel.

**1923** German scientist Herman Oberth publishes a book on the technical problems of space flight.

**1926** Robert Goddard

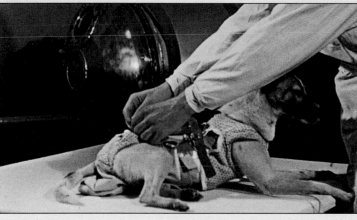

▲ Space dog Laika

launches the first liquid-propellant rocket.

**1942** A German A-4 rocket reaches a height of 60 miles.

**1957 October** The Soviet Union launches Sputnik 1, the first artificial satellite.

**November** Launch of Sputnik 2, with dog Laika.

**1958 January** First U.S. satellite, Explorer 1, launched.

**December** NASA launches first communications satellite.

**1961 April** Soviet cosmonaut Yuri Gagarin is the first man in space.

**May** Alan Shepard is the first American in space.

**1962 February** John Glenn is the first American to orbit the Earth.

**1963 June** Cosmonaut Valentina Tereshkova is the first woman in space.

**1964 October** Three cosmonauts orbit the earth in Voshkod 1.

**1965** NASA's first manned Gemini flight.

**July** U.S. probe Mariner 4 photographs Mars.

**1967 January** Three Apollo astronauts killed in launchpad fire.

**June** Soviet probe Venera 4 transmits data on Venus' atmosphere.

**1968 October** First manned Apollo flight.

**1969 July** Apollo

▲ Mercury crewmen

astronauts Neil Armstrong and Edwin "Buzz" Aldrin become the first men on the Moon.

**1971 May** Capsule from Soviet probe Mars 3 lands on Mars.

**November** NASA's probe Mariner 9 is the first to orbit Mars.

**1973 May** Skylab 2 launched with a crew of three.

**1975 July** NASA's Apollo spacecraft docks with a Soyuz spacecraft.

**October** Soviet probe Venera 9 lands on Venus and photographs the planet's surface.

**1976 July** Nasa's Viking 1 sends photographs from Mars.

**1977 August, September** NASA launches Voyagers 1 and 2.

**1981 April** Launch of Columbia, NASA's first space shuttle, with astronauts John Young and Robert Crippen.

**1983 June** U.S. probe Pioneer 10 becomes the first spacecraft to travel beyond all the planets.

**November** Spacelab, built by the European Space Agency (ESA) is first launched in the space shuttle.

**1986 January** Space shuttle Challenger explodes shortly after launch, killing its crew of seven.

**February** Launch of

▲ ESA shuttle *Hermes*

Soviet space station Mir.

**March** ESA's probe Giotto passes Halley's comet and sends data and photographs.

**1988 September** U.S. manned space programs resumed with launch of shuttle Discovery.

**November** Unmanned Soviet space shuttle Buran launches by Energia.

**1990** Hubble Space Telescope launched.

**1993 December** Space shuttle mission to repair faulty Hubble telescope is successful.

**1994** A variety of probes and satellites witness the collision between Jupiter and the Comet Shoemaker-Levy which creates several enormous fireballs.

**1995 July** Space shuttle Atlantis docks with Russian space station Mir.

# GLOSSARY

**Active suspension**
A computer-controlled system that keeps the car body at a fixed height above the ground by adjusting the suspension at each wheel.

**Aerofoil section**
The shape of an aircraft's wing when seen from the side, with a greater curvature on the upper surface which makes the air travel faster over the wing than below it, thus producing a lift.

**Ailerons**
Movable control surfaces, usually on the outer rear edges of the main wings, that make the plane roll (bank or tilt) to the left or to the right.

**Air bag**
A safety device mounted on the steering wheel. The bag inflates in the event of a collision, to prevent chest injuries to the driver.

**Anti-lock braking system (ABS)**
A computer-controlled braking system. ABS applies and releases brake pressure to individual wheels to prevent wheel lock and skidding in poor weather conditions.

**Ballast**
Heavy material, such as water or rock, used to make a ship more stable when it is not carrying cargo. Also water used to make a submarine submerge.

**Boiler**
A vessel in a steam engine where water is heated to produce the steam which expands in the cylinders.

**Booster**
A rocket engine strapped to a space craft to give it extra thrust during the first seconds after launch. It is usually jettisoned after use.

**Capacity**
Engine size, measured by the amount of air displaced by its cylinders during one cycle.

**Catalytic converter**
A special filter fitted to modern exhaust systems. It contains chemicals which remove pollutants from exhaust gases.

**Chassis**
The framework of a car, to which the engine, wheels and body are attached.

**Computer-Aided Design (CAD)**
A computerised system which aids the design of modern cars.

**Computer management**
A computer system now fitted to many high-performance cars. It monitors the engine and makes adjustments to maintain fuel efficiency.

**Cosmonaut**
The term for a space pilot used by Russia.

**Crankshaft**
The rod or shaft which converts the up and down (oscillating) movement of the pistons into a rotary (turning) movement to drive the wheels.

**Cylinder**
A vessel inside an engine where steam or ignited fuel expands, pushing a piston.

**Elevators**
Movable control surfaces, usually on the tailplane (small rear wings), that make the plane go up or down.

**Fuel injection**
A means of supplying the engine cylinders with extra fuel in accurate, controlled doses.

**Fuselage**
The main body of a plane, usually shaped like a long tube.

**Geostationary orbit**
A common flight path of satellites above the Earth's equator. A satellite in geostationary orbit keeps pace with the rotation of the Earth, appearing to hover over the same spot on the Earth's surface.

**Gyroscope**
A device containing a heavy, fast spinning wheel. The wheel resists changes in direction, so the gyroscope is used in automatic steering systems.

**Industrial Revolution**
The period from about 1750 to the late 1800's, when industry was born in Europe and America. One of the main innovations of the period was the steam engine.

**Keel**
A ridge running along the base of a hull, which gives the hull strength. Deep keels also help stop sailing ships drifting sideways.

# GLOSSARY

**Knocking**
Also known as pinking or detoning, is caused by faulty tuning of the engine. It occurs when the air-fuel mixture in the cylinders is igniting too early or too quickly, which makes a metallic "knock" or "pink."

**Launcher**
A launch vehicle, or rocket engine, that carries a payload into space.

**Module**
A section of craft that can be separated from other sections.

**Monocoque**
One-piece car chassis pioneered by Citroën in 1934.

**Oxidizer**
Substance containing oxygen that mixes with the fuel in a rocket engine and enables the fuel to burn.

**Payload**
A rocket's cargo, such as a satellite.

**Piston**
A block of metal which sits inside a cylinder in an engine. The piston moves in and out to turn a shaft.

**Pitch**
One of three directions of movements of an aircraft. It means to point up or down, so as to ascend or descend.

**Probe**
An unmanned spacecraft.

**Propellant**
The substance burned in a rocket engine to produce thrust.

**Radar**
An electronic system for locating objects by sending out radio waves and detecting the reflections - short for RAdio Detection and Ranging.

**Roll**
One of the three directions of movement of an aircraft. It means to tilt or bank to one side or the other, following a corkscrewlike path.

**Rotary-winged craft**
An aircraft in which the wings whirl round and round, such as a helicopter or autogyro.

**Rudder**
Movable control surface, usually on the rear of the fin, that makes the plane turn left or right.

**Safety cage**
A reinforced structure around the passenger compartment to reduce injury in a collision.

**Satellite**
An object orbiting a larger one. The Moon is a natural satellite of the Earth. There are now many artificial or man-made satellites orbiting the Earth.

**Self-righting**
A boat, such as a lifeboat, which rights itself if it capsizes. The cabin is watertight and the weight of the engine is low to make the boat stable.

**Sound barrier**
The speed of sound, which must be exceeded to fly supersonic. At sea level it is reached at about 761 mph (1,226 km/h).

**Stealth**
Technology in which a plane's shape and surface coverings are designed to minimize radio reflections and so make it less noticeable to radar.

**Strait**
A narrow sea channel which connects two different areas of seas or oceans.

**Thrust**
The pushing force generated by a rocket's engine.

**Thruster**
Small rocket motor used to make minor adjustments to a spacecraft's position.

**Transmission**
The system of gears and shafts which transmits the turning of the engine to the wheels.

**Turbocharger**
A pump driven by the engine's exhaust, which improves the fuel-air mixture fed to the cylinders, and so gives better engine performance.

**Turbofan**
A type of jet engine with a very large-bladed turbine or "fan" at the front.

**Yaw**
One of the three directions of movement of an aircraft. It means to swing to the left or right, like a car being turned left or right.

# INDEX

# INDEX

**Photographic credits:**
Airbus Industrie, BMW Cars, British Aerospace, British Shipbuilders, Charles de Vere, David Hardy, Dept. of Defense, Washington DC, Eye Ubiquitous, Ford Cars, Frank Spooner Pictures, Hoverspeed, Hughes Helicopters, Hulton Deutsch, Hutchison Library, Mary Evans Picture Library, NASA, McDonnell Douglas, National Museum Motor Museum at Beaulieu, Novosti RIA, P&O Cruises, Popperfoto, Princess Cruises, Quadrant Photo Library, Renault UK, Robert Harding Picture Library, Roger Vlitos, Rolls Royce, Science Museum Library, Science Photo Library, Shell Photo Services, Spectrum Colour Library, Valdagno Italia, Wartsila